BIOMIMICRY *in* ARCHITECTURE

Michael Pawlyn

RIBA Publishing

For Umi and Sol

MICHAEL PAWLYN BSc, BArch, RIBA, is Director of Exploration Architecture Ltd, where he focuses on environmentally sustainable projects that take their inspiration from nature. Prior to that, he worked with the firm Grimshaw for ten years and was central to the team that radically re-invented horticultural architecture for the Eden Project, being responsible for leading the design of the Warm Temperate and Humid Tropics Biomes and subsequent phases. He lectures widely on the subject of sustainable design in the UK and abroad.

© Michael Pawlyn, 2011

Published by RIBA Publishing,
15 Bonhill Street, London EC2P 2EA

ISBN 978 1 85946 375 8

Stock code 67855

First published 2011, reprinted 2012, 2013

British Library Cataloguing in Publications Data
A catalogue record for this book is available from the British Library.

Commissioning Editor: James Thompson
Project Editor: Neil O'Regan
Designed and typeset by Alex Lazarou
Printed and bound by W&G Baird

While every effort has been made to check the accuracy and quality of the information given in this publication, neither the Author nor the Publisher accept any responsibility for the subsequent use of this information, for any errors or omissions that it may contain, or for any misunderstandings arising from it.

RIBA Publishing is part of RIBA Enterprises Ltd.
www.ribaenterprises.com

Contents

Foreword: Jonathon Porritt

WHEN HISTORIANS come to look back on the twentieth century, from the vantage point of their genuinely sustainable society in the second half of this century, one of the most disputatious areas of enquiry will be fathoming out exactly why we did so little about 'sustainable living' in the second half of that century. It wasn't that we didn't have the knowledge, because we did. It wasn't that we didn't have the technology, because we could have. More mundanely, caught up as we were in our post-war cornucopian fantasies, we simply couldn't be arsed.

Broadly speaking, we were content with our model of consumption-driven economic growth, for all people, apparently forever, and just accepted the rising environmental damage as an acceptable price to pay for it.

Happily, we do at last seem to be waking up after these dismal decades of life-destroying arrogance. Illusions of the 'limitlessness' of the planet are evaporating as the ineluctable physical reality of scarcity impacts on more and more aspects of our economy. People no longer dismiss out of hand concerns about 'peak oil' or about diminishing supplies of critical raw materials.

And those control fantasies that once persuaded us that making war on nature would somehow turn out to be the best way of advancing humankind's special interests are giving way to a much more sophisticated understanding of the need for balance and reciprocity between ourselves and the rest of the living world.

Michael Pawlyn's fascinating work opens up one particularly intriguing aspect of that search for a new balance – biomimicry in architecture. He defines biomimicry as 'mimicking the functional basis of biological forms, processes and systems to produce sustainable solutions', and he invites us to explore not just its potential but specific case studies in architecture where biomimicry has already had an important influence.

I came away from reading this with the distinct impression that what's out there today, already *in situ*, provides just the tiniest insight into what lies ahead. Biomimicry is increasingly well established in the fields of industrial design, engineering and manufacturing, and even in medicine and fashion. The profession of architecture, however, has been slow to incorporate any of the basic principles – let alone the practice – of biomimicry into its teaching.

Most contemporary architects would be quick to attribute that to a lack of imagination on the part of their clients. However, there is a broader case to be made that relatively few architects have, as yet, used their professional skills and their standing in society to the full to help other people live more sustainably in buildings and spaces that are fit for purpose in a very different age.

Michael Pawlyn clearly feels much of that frustration himself, and is keen to demonstrate that even as architects become more mindful of the impact their work has on the environment, there is only so much they can do within the existing paradigm. If we remain stuck in a waste-generating, inherently polluting model of development (using raw materials in the 'heat, beat and treat paradigm', as Janine Benyus describes it), then we will only ever get to the 'less bad' (or 'less unsustainable' in my terms) in our use of the natural world – but never to good!

It's that entire paradigm that we have to render obsolete, designing out 'waste' as such by ensuring that as much as possible of what we create remains useful to us for as long as possible, in one way or another, and performs functionally with zero impact on the natural world. Biomimicry allows wealth-creators of every kind to emulate natural forms in their own work, using 'nature' as a critical sourcebook.

Happily, there's no shortage of role models. From the insect world alone, we are invited to learn from the mud-dauber wasp, compass termites, Eastern tent caterpillars, female bauble spiders and the extraordinary Namibian fog-basking beetle! Pawlyn introduces us to a veritable treasure trove of teachers. And at the heart of this celebration of evolution lies a wonderful paradox. Even as our politicians and economists focus ever more intently on the problems of scarcity (in terms of oil, land, water, precious metals, rare earths, and so on), we are only just beginning to appreciate the astonishing abundance with which we are surrounded.

In short, it's not the lack of biophysical plenty that will constrain the future of humankind, but rather the lack of vision and creativity on our part.

Jonathon Porritt

14 January 2011

Jonathon Porritt is Founder Director of Forum for the Future
www.forumforthefuture.org

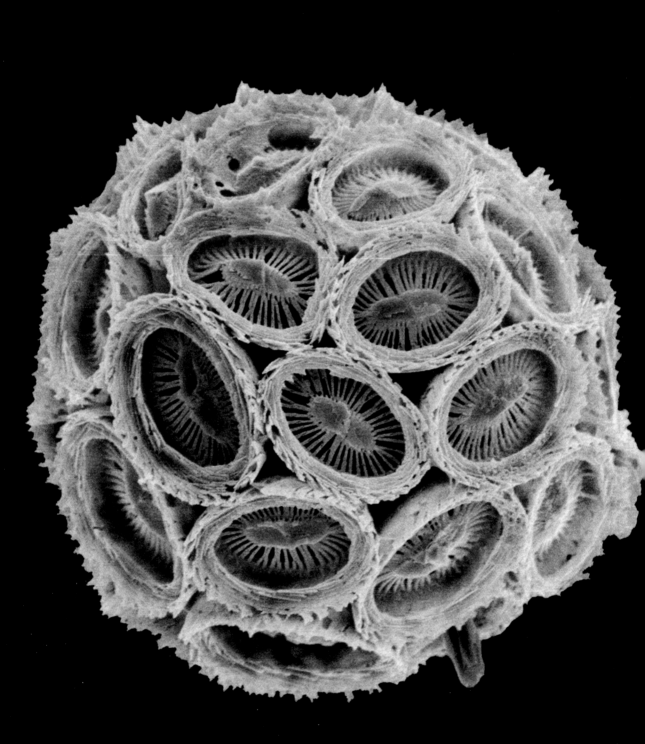

Introduction

You never change things by fighting the existing reality.
To change something, build a new model that makes the existing model obsolete.
RICHARD BUCKMINSTER FULLER

THIS IS A BOOK ABOUT SOLUTIONS. It is about learning from a source of ideas that has benefited from a 3.8-billion-year research and development period. That source is the vast array of species that inhabit the earth and represent evolutionary success stories. Biological organisms can be seen as embodying technologies that are equivalent to those invented by humans, and in many cases they have solved the same problems with a far greater economy of means. Humans have achieved some truly remarkable things, such as modern medicine and the digital revolution, but, when one sees some of the extraordinary adaptations that have evolved in natural organisms, it is hard not to feel a sense of humility about how much we still have to learn.

There are, I believe, three major changes that we need to bring about if the grand project of humanity is to endure: achieving radical increases in resource efficiency, shifting from a fossil-fuel economy to a solar economy and transforming from a linear, wasteful and polluting way of using resources to a completely closed-loop model in which all resources are stewarded in cycles and nothing is lost as waste. None of these will be easy but if we choose to embark on these linked journeys then there is, in my opinion, no better discipline than biomimicry to help reveal many of the solutions that we need.

1. Coccolithophores (marine micro-organisms) make their skeletons from calcium carbonate using elements in seawater and are thought to be part of the planet's long-term carbon cycle. In geological periods when carbon dioxide levels in the atmosphere have risen, coccolithophores bloomed and, when they died, fell to the ocean floor to form layers of limestone thus transferring carbon from the atmosphere to the lithosphere

Architecture and the natural world

Throughout history, architects have looked to nature for inspiration for building forms and approaches to decoration. This book aims to study one particular aspect of 'nature as sourcebook' that is distinct from the majority of architectural references to the natural world. The intention is to study ways of translating adaptations in biology into solutions in architecture. We are entering the Ecological Age, and it is the contention of this book that many of the lessons that we will need for this new era are to be found in nature itself.

What has been commonly called 'The Industrial Revolution' (but could also be referred to as 'The Fossil Fuel Age') could now be seen as a diversion from the kind of ingenuity that we once had in common with nature's evolved solutions. The ubiquity and convenience of fossil fuels has allowed extreme inefficiency to develop, and has effectively undermined resourcefulness. The lessons from nature which informed many vernacular approaches to design and manufacturing were therefore abandoned and largely lost from our collective memory. Now that the folly of releasing many millennia of stored carbon is becoming increasingly apparent, there is an opportunity to explore the incredible effectiveness of the responses that natural organisms have evolved. For virtually every problem that we currently face – whether it is producing energy, finding fresh water or manufacturing benign materials – there will be numerous examples in nature that we could benefit from studying. While fascination with nature undoubtedly goes back as long as human existence itself, now we have an opportunity to revisit the idea of learning from biology with massive advantages of scientific knowledge, better tools and aesthetic sensibilities unconstrained by historical dogma. There are few times when designers have been presented with such an opportunity.

Many current approaches to environmentally sustainable architecture are based on mitigation. The suggestion from the examples collected in this book is that it is possible to go further than this, and for buildings and cities to be regenerative. In some cases, buildings will cease to be static consumers and can become nett producers of useful resources. The intention is therefore to transcend the mimicking of natural forms and attempt to understand the principles that lie behind those forms and systems. Then we can look for opportunities to create works of architecture that are celebratory as well as being radically more resource efficient.

What do we mean by 'biomimicry'?

The term 'biomimicry' first appeared in scientific literature in 1962,[1] and grew in usage particularly amongst materials scientists in the 1980s. Some scientists preferred the term 'biomimetics' or, less frequently, 'bionics'. There has been an enormous surge of interest during the last ten years, brought about to a large extent by individuals like biological-sciences writer Janine Benyus, Professor of Biology Steven Vogel and Professor of Biomimetics Julian Vincent, who have all written extensively in this subject area. Julian Vincent defines it as 'the abstraction of good design from nature',[2] while for Janine Benyus it is 'The conscious emulation of nature's genius'.[3] The only significant difference between 'biomimetics' and 'biomimicry' is that many users of the latter intend it to be specifically focused on developing sustainable solutions, whereas the former can be, and on occasions has been, applied to fields of endeavour such as military technology. I will be using biomimicry and biomimetics as essentially synonymous, and I like to define the discipline as 'mimicking the functional basis of biological forms, processes and systems to produce sustainable solutions'.

There are two other terms that are worth clarifying: firstly 'bio-utilisation' and secondly 'biophilia'.

Bio-utlisation refers to the direct use of nature for beneficial purposes, such as incorporating planting in and around buildings to produce evaporative cooling. We will see later in Chapter 3 that this approach has a major role to play in biomimetic systems thinking. Biophilia was a term popularised by the biologist E. O. Wilson, and refers to a hypothesis that there is an instinctive bond between human beings and other living organisms.[4]

From an architectural perspective there is an important distinction to be made between 'biomimicry' and 'biomorphism'. Modern architects have frequently used nature as a source for unconventional forms and for symbolic association. There are some examples of how this has produced majestic works of architecture, such as Eero Saarinen's TWA terminal (fig. 2) and Frank Lloyd Wright's Johnson Wax building (fig. 3). In the esoteric realm, Le Corbusier used allusions to natural forms extensively for their associated symbolism (fig. 4). The reason that it is necessary to make a distinction is because we require a functional revolution of sorts if we are to bring about the transformations described above, and I firmly believe that it will be biomimicry rather than biomorphism that will deliver the solutions we need.

Are there grey areas between biomorphism and biomimicry? There are certainly projects that have been based on a very detailed understanding of natural forms and have used this to great effect. The key, I believe, is whether the design engages with the function delivered by a particular natural adaptation. If it does, then it is fair to label it as biomimetic; if it does not, then I think it is correct to say it is biomorphic.

I do not want to sound too dismissive of biomorphic architecture. It is quite possible for the two approaches to coexist in one building, and biomorphism can add further meaning than would be achieved from a purely technical use of biomimicry. It is also worth considering the limitations of biomimicry. Just as with any design discipline, it will not automatically produce good architecture, and we should be wary of trying to become purely scientific about design. Architecture should always have an emotional dimension – it should touch the spirit, it should be uplifting and it should celebrate the age in which it was created.

2

3

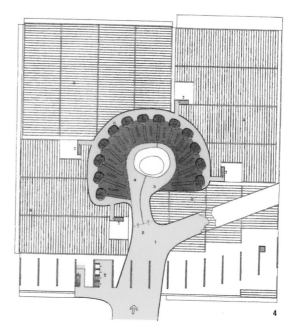

4

2. The TWA terminal at John F Kennedy Airport, New York, in which Eero Saarinen used biomorphic forms to capture the poetry of flight

3. Frank Lloyd Wright likened the columns in the Johnson Wax building to water lilies and, while they create a spectacular space, they have nothing functionally in common with lily leaves

4. Le Corbusier, possibly the greatest symbolist architect of all time, appears to have made deliberate reference to the cleansing function of kidneys in the design of the washrooms for the unbuilt Olivetti Headquarters project

There are some cases in which a biological example may already have some of these inspiring qualities – one could cite the Amazon water lilies that were translated into concrete beauty by Pier Luigi Nervi. In other cases, such as the principles of structural efficiency revealed in abalone shells, it is no more (or less) than a promising starting point from which to imagine all manner of spaces with, for instance, the magical qualities of Eladio Dieste's architecture (fig. 5).

The word 'natural' is used in many contexts to imply some kind of inherent virtue or 'rightness', and it would be easy to misconstrue biomimicry as being about the pursuit of solutions that are 'more natural'.[5] This is not the aim. There are certain aspects of nature that we definitely do not want to emulate – voracious parasitism to name just one. There is also a danger in romanticising nature. What I believe nature does hold that is of enormous value is a vast array of products (for want of a better word) that have benefited from an extremely long and ruthless process of selection and refinement. Evolution could be summarised as a process based on genetic variability, from which the fittest are selected over time. The pressures of survival have driven organisms into some almost unbelievably specific ecological niches and into developing astonishing adaptations to resource-constrained environments. The relevance of this to the constraints that humans will face in the decades ahead is obvious. We will, in the chapters of this book, study a beetle that can harvest fresh water from the air in a desert environment, a reptile that effectively drinks with its feet and another beetle that can detect a forest fire at a distance of 10 km.[6] We will also learn about projects that achieve alchemical transformations of waste into highly productive systems.

5

Origins of biomimicry

While there is no proof, it is quite likely that the forms
of eggs inspired the first human-made domes, and in
this sense biomimicry is far from being a recent idea.
Leonardo da Vinci was clearly a pioneer, and his visions
were hundreds of years ahead of his contemporaries.
Other examples abound, as Steven Vogel has clearly
described in *Cat's Paws and Catapults*.[7] Around 1719,
the production of paper shifted from using cotton
and linen fibres after the French entomologist Réne-
Antoine Réamur suggested that wasps' use of wood
pulp demonstrated an alternative. In the field of naval
architecture there are examples such as that of Sir
George Cayley, who in 1809 studied the streamlined
form of dolphins and trout in order to develop ship
hulls with lower coefficients of drag.

More recently there are some well-documented
examples such as the invention of Velcro around 1948,
and in the last decade there has been a phenomenal
flourishing of biomimicry as more and more designers
respond to the demand for sustainable products.
The Mercedes biomimetic concept car (fig. 8) is
inspired by the surprisingly streamlined and roomy
boxfish (fig. 7), Olympic swimsuits based on shark
skin (fig. 9) and new types of drill designed after a
wood wasp's ovipositor[8] have all delivered a superior
product by learning from the functions delivered by
adaptations in natural organisms.

To date, biomimicry has only been applied to
building design to a fairly limited extent, often relying
on frequently cited examples such as termite mounds
and spider webs. In recent years, biomimicry has
developed very rapidly in other fields such as industrial
design and medicine. This book will explore the
potential that biomimicry offers to architecture. It is
not intended to be an exhaustive survey of works of
architecture that are biomimetic, but it does aspire to
be a comprehensive sourcebook to encourage other
architects and students to explore a wonderfully rich
range of solutions.

6

5. The Iglesia Christa Obero designed by Eladio Dieste
6. Burdock burrs were the source of inspiration for
    George de Mestral – the Swiss engineer who
    invented Velcro. Apparently after some recent
    frustration with zips, he noticed the way that
    burdock burrs clung to his dog's coat and, after
    studying them with a magnifying glass, designed
    the first version of the now ubiquitous fastening

7 + 8

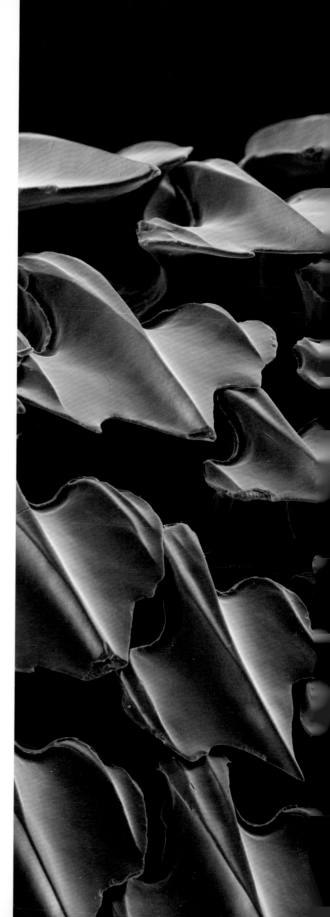

7. The boxfish

8. In spite of its rather cubic form the boxfish has a very low coefficient of drag and inspired the designers of the new Mercedes

9. Sharks and other elasmobranchs have a very rough skin texture (as this scanning electron microscope image of spiny dogfish skin shows) which, somewhat counter-intuitively, creates a more streamlined surface. New biomimietic swimsuits based on shark skin were so successful in allowing swimmers to move faster through the water that they were banned by FINA the governing body for world swimming

Chapter ONE

How can we build more efficient structures?

MUCH OF THIS CHAPTER could be captured in a single phrase by Julian Vincent who has observed that in nature 'materials are expensive and shape is cheap' as opposed to technology, where the opposite tends to be the case.[9] Nature makes extremely economical use of materials, and this is normally achieved through evolved ingenuity of form. Using folding, vaulting, ribs, inflation and other measures, natural organisms have created effective forms that demonstrate astonishing efficiency. The many manifestations of this efficiency provide a rich sourcebook of ideas for structures that could be radically more efficient than those found in conventional human-made architecture.

Why is nature this way? The pressures of survival in all its varied aspects – finding sustenance, thermo-regulating, mating and avoiding predation, amongst many other factors – have, over aeons, ruthlessly refined the structures, and other adaptations that genetic mutation and recombination has created. The process continues of course, but we can observe in nature today many of the best structures evolved throughout the history of life on earth. So, following the 'less materials – more design' paradigm, we will explore an array of examples showing how a minimum of material can be used to maximum effect.

Simple transformations of materials into structural elements

If one takes a square cross-section of solid material with a side dimension 24 mm (fig. 11), it will have the same bending resistance as a circular solid section of diameter 25 mm with only 81.7 per cent of the material.[10] Similarly, a hollow tube with only 20 per cent of the material of the solid square can achieve the same stiffness. In engineering terms, material has been removed from areas close to the neutral axis and placed where it can deliver much greater resistance to bending – achieving the same result but with a fraction of the material.

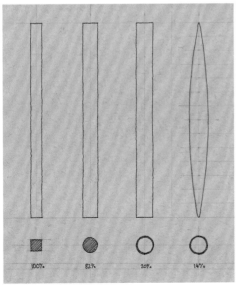

10. X-ray image of an Amazon water lily leaf showing an example of how robust structures are created in nature with a minimum of materials. The network of ribs stiffen the large area of leaf without adding excessive thickness
11. Sketch showing how four equally stiff structural elements can be made with varying degrees of efficiency. By using shape and putting the material where it needs to be it is possible to use only 14% of the material of a solid square section. (After Adriaan Beukers and Ed van Hinte, Lightness – the Inevitable renaissance of minimum energy structures)

12

13

Nature is abundant in examples that demonstrate this structural principle: hollow bones, plant stems and feather quills to name just a few. One of the most accomplished demonstrations can be found in bamboo, some species of which grow to 40 m tall. Bamboo (fig 12) displays another method by which circular hollow section elements can be strengthened, and that is through regular nodes which act like bulkheads. A tubular element fails under loading through one side of the tube collapsing in towards the central axis, leading to overall buckling. The nodes provide great resistance to such structural failure, and are part of what has facilitated bamboo's lofty accomplishments. So why aren't more trees hollow tubes? In taxonomic terms, bamboo is actually a species of grass – a damned successful one, but a grass nevertheless! Trees are different in that they generally create a canopy of cantilevering branches rather than a multiplicity of stems. We will come back to tree trunks, which, as solid cross-sectional forms, may appear to contradict the principle of placing material where it does the most work.

Whereas bamboo is a relatively pure embodiment of tubular structural engineering, bones are more complex and frequently reveal ways in which asymmetrical forces are resolved in the process of conducting loads down to the ground. Figure 14 shows the lines of

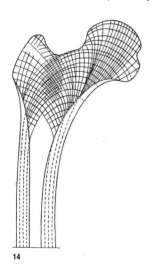

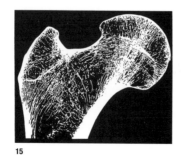

14

15

16

force through a femur, and figure 15 shows an X-ray image of the same bone. What we see is a precise match between the density of bone filaments and the concentration of stresses; where there is high stress there is a proliferation of material, and where there is no stress there is a void. There are some extreme cases in which intense selective pressure to achieve high strength with minimal weight has yielded impressive results. As D'Arcy Thompson's *On Growth and Form* documented, the vulture's metacarpal (fig. 16) is identical to a Warren truss, using struts and ties to create structural depth between top and bottom chords.

Transformations of planar surfaces

One of the simplest ways of transforming a planar surface into something that provides protection is to roll it in a similar manner to the structures made by the Cherry leaf roller caterpillar, and within which it carries out its metamorphosis. Shuhei Endo used a similar trick for his public washroom building in Singu-cho Park, Japan (fig. 17), rolling a sheet material into a form that encloses a series of spaces, although the process accommodated is not quite as elevated as the caterpillar's.

Plants have had to evolve ways to present large amounts of photosynthetic surface in order to absorb light. Growing bigger leaves by increasing their thickness has significant drawbacks, so curves and folds are incorporated to create stiffer elements out of thin material. In the case of the Southern Magnolia, the fold occurs along the midrib and each half of the leaf is curved. Both the fold and the curve contribute to the leaf's stiffness. In rainforest environments, daylight at forest-floor level is scarce and many plants have responded with large leaves folded into fan forms.

Architects Tonkin Liu, working with structural engineer Ed Clark at Arup, were inspired by the forms of various seashells and techniques from tailoring to develop a new form of construction derived from planar surfaces, which they refer to as a 'shell-lace structure' (fig 18 & 19). Just as with the molluscs, the structure derives its strength from a combination of curves, folds and ribs so that large forms can be created using extremely thin sheet material. New structural-analysis software allows a high degree of refinement, and identifies low-stress locations where perforations can be made to further reduce the amount of material. The end product is an extremely elegant structure, constructed with a minimum of materials, that derives its strength from its form rather than mass.

12. The regular nodes in the stems of bamboo act like bulkheads stiffening the tube and preventing the normal way in which tubular structures fail - the wall collapsing in towards the centre leading to overall bending

13. The 'Hex-tri-hex' structure used of the Eden Project was originally developed by Max Mengeringhausen who was inspired by the tube / node structure of bamboo

14. Diagram showing lines of stress passing through a bone

15. X-ray through a bone showing arrangement of boney trabeculae

16. As a result of intense selective pressure for lightness, some birds have evolved remarkably efficient structural forms like this Vulture's metacarpal which is effectively identical to a Warren truss

17. Washroom building in Singu-cho Park, designed by architect Shuhei Endo, showing a simple transformation of a planar surface into an enclosure

17

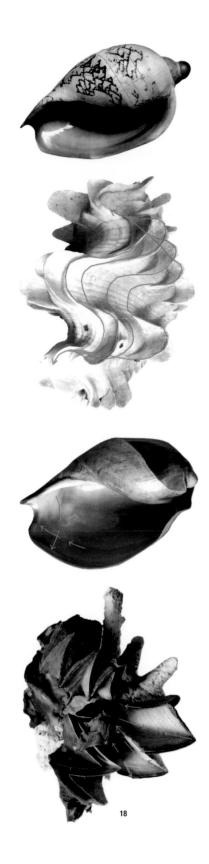

18

18. Diagrams by Tonkin Liu Architects showing how structural principles from shells were analysed

19. The Shi Ling bridge designed by architects Tonkin Liu and structural engineer Ed Clark of Arup. An example of a 'Shell-lace structure', that achieves efficiency of materials by exploiting vaulted, folded and twisted forms from shells

Large-span structures by Pier-Luigi Nervi

One of the most stunning biological examples of stiffening is to be found in the giant Amazon water lily (*Victoria amazonica*). Leaves of up to three metres in diameter with smooth top surfaces are strengthened on their undersides by a radial, branching, network of ribs. The brilliant structural engineer Pier Luigi Nervi closely studied corrugations in nature, and may well have used the Amazon water lily as a source of inspiration for his Palazzetto dello Sport (fig. 20) in Rome and his unbuilt project for the Centre National des Industries et Techniques. Both schemes employed the principle of using ribs to give effective structural depth to a thin planar surface, combined with the benefits of dome / shell action. In the Palazzetto dello Sport, radial bifurcating ribs reduce the distance over which the outer surface must span. The outer surface in turn connects all the ribs together, so loads are more evenly distributed.

One of the challenges for architects and engineers in trying to emulate natural forms has been in achieving efficiency through complexity of form without adding excessive cost. While nature manufactures things molecule by molecule, human artefacts are constrained by the practical and economic limitations of our construction technology. For Nervi the miracle material that allowed him to achieve his aims was reinforced concrete, about which he said 'The very fact of not having at its origin a form of its own . . . permits it to adapt itself to any form and to constitute resisting organisms',[11] and 'Concrete is a living creature which can adapt itself to any form, need or stress'.[12] We see also in these statements his use of biological terminology to describe engineered structures, and there is a sense in which his structures capture both muscular and skeletal qualities. In many of his designs we see the forces that are resolved made manifest in the forms of the structure. For example, the ribs and downstand beams in his Gatti Wool Factory of 1953 precisely follow the lines of principal stresses.

Nervi was a revolutionary not just in the way that he rejected the 'art versus science' dichotomy of his age but also in his technological innovation. A key breakthrough was his invention of 'ferro-cemento' – a thin, flexible, elastic and very strong material composed of several layers of fine steel mesh sprayed with cement mortar. It can stand great strains without cracking and, because of its superior strength and elasticity, can be used in exceedingly thin slabs and shells. Nervi pioneered the use of plaster moulds for the *ferro-cemento* which resulted in clean smooth surfaces that required no additional finishing. This eliminated the need for timber formwork and the rectilinear constraints that it imposed. For the Palazzetto dello Sport all the *ferro-cemento* elements were prefabricated in units that were less than 40 mm thick. Once craned into position, protruding steel bars from each adjacent unit were welded together and grouted to create a former for the in-situ concrete, which unified the whole structure.

Many of Nervi's projects were won in competitions, and the secret to his success was his frequent ability to produce the most cost-effective schemes. In a satisfying parallel with the refining process of evolution, his combination of ingenuity and biomimicry led to a remarkable efficiency of resources.

20. The structural engineering genius Pier-Luigi Nervi frequently used examples from nature to inspire more efficient structures as in this example of the Palazzetto dello Sport that has a striking resemblance to the leaves of the giant Amazon water lily

Shells and domes

Nature is an accomplished maker of shells and domes. One such builder, whose specifications have been thoroughly scrutinised is the abalone (fig. 21). It has evolved a shell which electron microscopy reveals to be made of polygons of aragonite, a form of calcium carbonate, bonded together with a flexible polymer mortar. The composite action of these two substances forms a material stronger than the toughest human-made ceramics. Whereas we tend to make homogeneous materials through which a crack, once started, readily propagates, nature has evolved a matrix of hard 'platelets' with phenomenal resistance to cracking. Each platelet creates a point at which a crack stops and must then start afresh on a new platelet if it is to continue through the material. A degree of flexibility in the polymer helps to spread concentrated loads over a larger area of shell. This approach is already being pursued by materials scientists in order to make tougher car-body panels.

There is a vernacular method of construction called Guastavino vaulting (fig. 22) that has interesting parallels with the abalone and recently experienced a return to favour. This technique, named after the Valencian architect and builder Rafael Guastavino (1842–1908), involves, at its simplest, building a lower layer of terracotta tiles out from a circular concrete ring beam. This can be achieved without formwork as a plaster of Paris mortar is used, from which the tiles absorb moisture rapidly enough to form a good bond after half a minute. A second layer of tiles laid at a diagonal is applied on top with a stronger cement mortar, and then a third layer at the opposite diagonal. The result is an extremely strong shell structure that can span large distances and can be worked into a rich variety of forms. Clearly this is a form of construction that existed long before we knew about the detailed structure of the abalone. You might argue that the Guastavino vaulting is therefore not biomimetic. Well fine, but I think it is a case of accidental similarity that could nevertheless be further developed with lessons

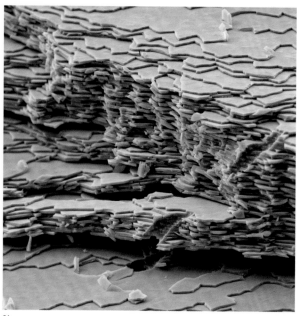

21

21.   A scanning electron micrograph showing the series of calcium carbonate discs that form an Abalone shell
22.   Mapungubwe Interpretation Centre designed by Peter Rich Architects using Guastavino vaulting
23.   The Wood Green Gridshell by Exploration. By using small sections of timber in a highly efficient form, gridshells can achieve factor 15 savings in resource use

22

from nature. We could potentially use a flexible mortar to increase its crack resistance and spanning capabilities. We could also form corrugations to push spanning distances even further while using minimal quantities of material. The potential is too great to quibble about its biological credentials.

Timber gridshells (fig. 23) could have been included in the section above about transformations of planar surfaces – indeed, they are often built by starting with a flat grid and then distorting it into shape. However, the structural aim is not to form a stiffened plane but to get a series of linear elements – usually wood – to act together as a shell. Domes and shells were almost undoubtedly first inspired by studying natural examples. Anyone who has tried to crush an egg by squeezing it lengthways between forefinger and thumb can testify to the robustness of a shell form. The elegance of gridshells shows what can be achieved by using ingenuity rather than brute force.[13]

As Mario Salvadori has observed, domes could be regarded as a continuous series of arches arranged in a circle and joined monolithically.[14] The engineering advantages become clear when one looks at the ratio of thickness to radius. For an arch this ratio is typically between 1:20 and 1:30, whereas for a dome it is between 1:200 and 1:300. Little wonder then, that this highly efficient form of construction has manifested itself in biological examples as diverse as microorganisms, seed pods, carapaces and skulls.

23

The Eden Project Humid Tropics and Warm Temperate Biomes

The most difficult challenges often hold the potential for the most inventive solutions. This is an adage that all architects learn as students, and the Eden Project, by Grimshaw, is perhaps as potent a demonstration of this as one could find. The brief called for the world's biggest greenhouse and the site was a huge china-clay pit – 90 m deep, hundreds of metres across and, in places, very unstable. To make matters more difficult, the site was still being quarried and there was no certainty about its ultimate shape.

The first design exercise was to establish which would be the best parts of the site for the building to inhabit. In spite of the challenges, the site had some great benefits – it created a sheltered microclimate and a series of south-facing slopes against which the building could be placed in order to maximise passive solar gain. To resolve the challenges of the irregular site, one of the members of the team, David Kirkland, proposed a radical solution inspired by soap bubbles (fig. 24) – a genuine Eureka moment. The idea was to create a string of bubbles, the diameters of which could be varied to provide the right growing heights in the different parts of the building, and to connect these along a 'necklace' line that could be arranged to suit the approximate topography. The team explored lots of different iterations of this bubble string and set them into 3D terrain models of the site. By cutting away everything that was below ground, the team arrived at the first images that resembled the final scheme.

The next challenge was to strive for the lightest possible structure. Studying a whole series of natural examples – from carbon molecules and single-celled animals such as radiolaria through to pollen grains – revealed that the most efficient way of structuring a spherical form is with a geodesic arrangement of pentagons and hexagons. Richard Buckminster Fuller pioneered this technology, and even has a form of carbon molecule (the 'Buckminster Fullerene') named after him. The design started with conservative structural assumptions and then set about refining the system. The most significant move in this process came in trying to maximise the size of the hexagons so that light penetration could be increased. Glass would have been a serious constraint, both in terms of its unit sizes and weight, so the team explored a material which had been used on some much smaller and more conventional buildings but that showed great potential.

Ethylene tetraflouroethylene (ETFE) is a high-strength polymer that can be formed into an ultra-lightweight cladding element by welding the edges of three layers together and then inflating it for stiffness. The great advantage of this was that it was one per cent of the weight of glass (a factor-100 saving) and could be made in much larger 'pillows' than the biggest available sheets of safety glass. A combination of wind-tunnel exploration and thorough material testing allowed the design of the enclosure to be tuned to the specific conditions of the site. A positive cycle of design occurred, in which one breakthrough facilitated another: with such large pillows it meant there was less steel, which in turn admitted more sunlight and reduced the amount of heat that would be needed in the colder times of the year. Less steel also produced substantial savings in substructure. The process of design refinement, resulted in a scheme that used a fraction of the resources of a conventional approach and cost a third of the normal rate for a glasshouse. The weight of the superstructure for the Humid Tropics Biome (fig. 25) is less than the weight of the air inside the building. If the team were to tackle the same challenge again, with more advanced materials technology and learning further lessons from biology, it is likely that further radical increases in resource efficiency could be achieved.

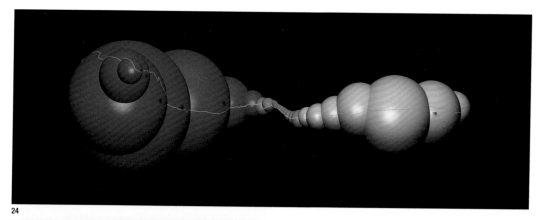

24

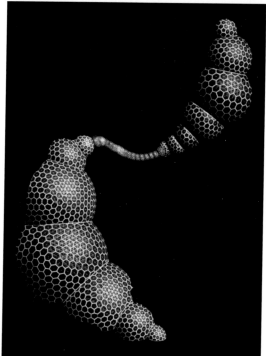

25a

25b

24. An early computer model developed by the Grimshaw team when conceiving of The Eden Project as a string of bubbles to be set into the irregular site

25. (a) Computer generated image showing the sections of geodesic structure of the bubbles that protruded above the ground; and (b) the interior of the Humid Tropics Biome at The Eden Project

In contrast to many of the historical precedents that were studied, the biomimetic approach resulted in a much more sympathetic relationship with the landscape. Examples such as the Palm House at Kew – a highly symmetrical building on a flattened site – can be read as an expression of the view of nature that prevailed at the time, as something that could be dominated by man. The Eden Project Biomes accommodated the existing form of the site with a minimum of excavation, and suggest a more respectful reconciliation between humans and the natural world.

Skeletons

As demonstrated by the vulture metacarpal described above, birds have evolved in response to particularly intense selective pressure on reducing weight. They are therefore a particularly good example of the 'materials are expensive and shape is cheap' maxim. Bird skulls (fig. 26), such as those of crows and magpies, are little short of engineering miracles. The effective thickness of the skull is increased while weight is decreased by creating multiple surfaces connected by a matrix of ties and struts – an astounding combination of shell action with space-frame technology, and all in a humble magpie.

This principle was the inspiration for a canopy structure (fig. 27) designed by architect Andres Harris.[15] The design was the result of a detailed understanding of the way in which bone tissue forms around pneumatised cells to create air voids between solid surfaces. The potential existed to construct the canopy in a way that was very similar to nature – using a web of inflated void formers, around which concrete, or eventually a more sophisticated material, could be cast.

Skeletons have been a source of inspiration for architects ever since D'Arcy Thompson published *On Growth and Form*, and demonstrated the parallels between structures such as the Forth Road Bridge and the form of dorsal vertebrae found in a horse. Engineer Jane Wernick, and architects Marks and Barfield, pursued similar interests in the design of their 'Bridge of the Future' (fig. 28), in which a series of steel interpretations of vertebrae is connected with tie rods to form an elegant spanning structure.

Another architect renowned for his love of skeletal structures is Santiago Calatrava, who has created many of the most graceful bridges in the world. While his exuberance is enjoyable, there is a sense in which

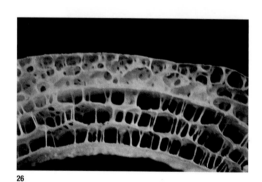

26

26.   Bird skull

27.   Canopy structure, designed by architect Andres Harris, using the same structural principles as bird skulls

28.   Bridge of the future by architects Marks Barfield and engineer Jane Wernick using steel tendons and vertebrae forms

29.   Biomorphic exuberance in the Milwaukee Art Museum by Santiago Calatrava

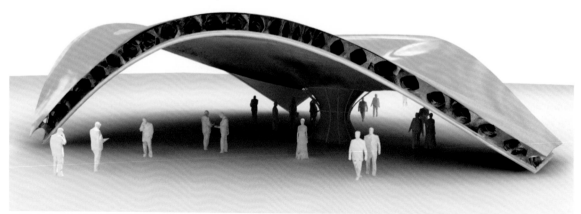

27

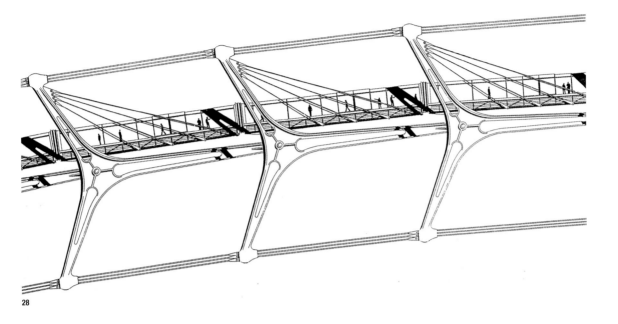

the biomorphic extravagance occasionally occludes a rational structural basis for the schemes (fig. 29). The beauty to be found in nature is often derived from its economy – the absence of the superfluous is part of the rigour that we perceive.

Our understanding of skeletons and how lessons from skeletal forms can be applied to engineering has developed enormously in recent years, particularly with the work of Claus Mattheck.[16] In nature, biological forms follow a simple rule that he describes as 'the axiom of uniform stress': In locations of stress concentration, material is built up until there is enough to evenly distribute the forces; in unloaded areas there is no material. The result approaches perfect efficiency, in which there is no waste material and all the material that exists is carrying its fair share of the load.

With his team at Karlsruhe Research Centre, Mattheck developed a design methodology that utilises two software processes (fig. 30) to create forms of biological design that are effectively identical to the refinements found in nature. The program allows designers to subject a rough structural computer model to the kind of forces that would be experienced in reality, which, depending on location, could include snow, wind and seismic loading as well as loads imposed by the building's use. The first stage uses 'Soft Kill Option' (SKO) software to eliminate material in zones where is little, or no, stress. Then a 'Computer Aided Optimisation' (CAO) programme refines the shapes and, where necessary, builds up material at the junctions to minimise the potential for stress concentrations that could lead to failure. Mattheck likens this process to starting with a roughly axed piece of timber, which is then carved to the near-final shape (the SKO stage) before being sanded and polished (CAO). The results can be surprisingly organic in form, and far more efficient than standard constructional shapes. Mercedes used this to develop the exoskeleton design for its boxfish-inspired car (fig. 31 & 32). We could do the same with buildings, and achieve huge increases in material efficiency while producing more elegant and structurally legible forms.

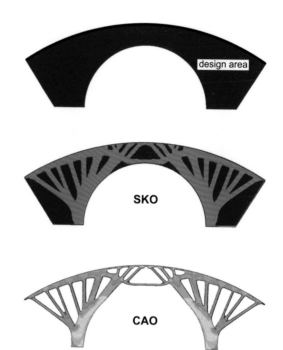

SKO

CAO

30

30. Diagram showing Claus Matheck's design refinement process using 'Softkill Option' (SKO) and Computer Aided Optimisation (CAO) software

31. Boxfish car – model showing the frame optimized with SKO and CAO software

32. Boxfish car – aerodynamic model

33. Coexistence Tower by Future Systems. The compression core and the helical arrangement of tension members around the perimeter has functional similarities with the structure of tree trunks

34. Trees growing in the shallow soils of rainforests have evolved buttress roots that resist overturning

Trees

Trees are also a focus of Mattheck's research, as they demonstrate the same stress uniformity and, perhaps even more clearly than bones, the idea of optimised junction shapes that avoid stress concentrations and can adapt over time. In human-made structures it is common for all the elements to be sized to resist the most onerous stress conditions that occur in only a few locations. The drawback is that in all other locations the structure is oversized and wasteful. In trees, material is grown at the branching points in a shape that analysis has shown to be the optimum form for even distribution of stress. Over the course of the tree's life the loads will change, and it is able to adapt constantly to these conditions.

The key difference between trees and bones is that in the former material cannot be removed, whereas in bone tissue it can be. Trees consequently grow as solid forms. This might seem surprising, given the hollowness of many bones. The explanation probably lies in the fact that there is not the same selective pressure for lightness in stationary trees as there is in animals that must move at speed to either catch, or avoid becoming, prey. One other possible explanation is that the solid core of trees is used to some extent as a compression core to resist the tension created by the outer sapwood, which grows in helical patterns up and around the trunk. This structural form has some similarities with Future Systems' Coexistence Tower (fig. 33). Bamboo, of course, has evolved hollow stems, but followed a different evolutionary path to trees in that it grows multiple stems without heavily cantilevered branches.

The root forms of trees could also inspire new approaches to creating foundations for buildings. The formation of a wide, stiff base effectively moves the pivot point some distance from the trunk and, on the opposite side, a branching network of roots mobilises a vast amount of soil as ballast to resist overturning.[17] In rainforests, where soils can be relatively shallow and therefore cannot provide the same resistance as those in more temperate climates, trees have evolved pronounced buttresses (fig. 34), which provide even greater resistance to overturning.[18]

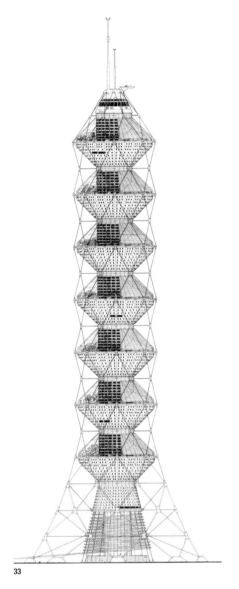

33

34

Webs / tension structures

Webs built by spiders have inspired a number of modern architects and engineers. Their forms range from the commonplace webs created by household spiders to the bizarre constructions of the female bauble spider (fig. 35) (*Achaearanea globispira*).[19]

Arguably, there is no greater champion of tension structures than the German architect and engineer Frei Otto (b.1925). He pioneered cable-net buildings and, through the Institute for Lightweight Structures that he established, has published 36 volumes on structural design principles derived from nature.[20] These books describe, in exhaustive detail, a vast array of natural inspiration, from radiolaria to skeletons, trees and indeed spiders' webs. While such finely engineered natural structures as spiders' webs may seem an obvious choice for direct translation into structures for human use, the designer quite quickly runs into problems. If a web gets damaged in a storm, one imagines that the spider doesn't get particularly grumpy about it and would get on with repairs straight afterwards. An architect's client would probably demonstrate less *sang-froid*. Spiders will happily digest lengths of silk thread and recycle it into new strands in a constant maintenance programme; we have to allow for more mundane approaches to repair. Further frustration comes in the form of practicalities such as acceptable deflections; while spiders will tolerate huge deflections, humans and cladding systems won't.

The end result is that the tension structures we achieve can look considerably less elegant than those made by arachnids. This is not to take anything away from Otto's buildings, such as the West German Pavilion at Expo 1967 (fig. 36), which are poetic and beautiful, but only to highlight some of the obstacles that biomimicry can present.

The most common form of tension structure is a cable net, which generally involves a series of guyed masts from which the web is suspended. Although they use more substantial vertical elements than Otto's tent-type schemes, Kenzo Tange's brilliant Olympic

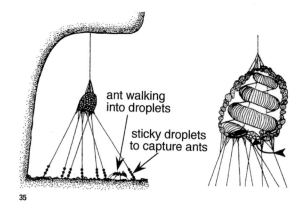

ant walking into droplets

sticky droplets to capture ants

35

stadia in Tokyo are essentially the same. The Grimshaw team, for the proposed third climatic enclosure at the Eden Project, pursued a different approach. The imperative design requirement for this enclosure was for it to achieve the highest possible light levels. This led the team to explore an approach that placed the heavier compression members around the perimeter of the building, while over the growing area the most minimal arrangement of tension members would be stretched. The Dry Tropics Biome (fig. 37) used a distorted lattice ring beam to form an anticlastic surface,[21] such that at any point on the surface the cables, and the membrane that they support, would be tensioned in two directions for maximum resistance to wind loading.

35. House of the female bauble spider apparently under the influence of Bruce Goff

36. The West German Pavilion at Expo 1967, Montreal by Frei Otto – perhaps the closest we have come to the elegance of spider's webs

37. The Eden Project Dry Tropics Biome by Grimshaw. The scheme aimed to maximise light levels inside by using a ring beam to stretch a minimal web of cables over the growing area

36

37

Pneumatic structures

A leaf, generally speaking, has very little woody tissue in it and relies instead for its stiffness on pressurised cell membranes. Plants use energy to accumulate sugars in their cells, which promotes the in-flow of water and consequently internal pressure. The force of all the cells pressing against each other is what keeps the leaf rigid and explains why plants wilt when short of water. The effect is similar to a fully inflated lilo that is strong enough to stand upright or span as a cantilever.

Adopting ideas from nature and increasing the scale of the objects involved can yield problems, because surface areas increase by a squared ratio and volumes increase by a cubed ratio. Put simply, this means that certain things that work on a small scale in nature would not work on a large scale because they would be far too heavy. This certainly applies to plant cells and the way that they rely on hydrostatic pressure. Fortunately, very similar effects can be achieved with membranes pressurised by air.

As architect Judit Kimpian has described in her dissertation 'PneuMatrix – the Architecture of Pneumatic Structures in the Digital World', air-supported constructions have had a somewhat chequered history. Firstly revolutionising the design of vehicle wheels, then adopted for numerous military purposes during the First and Second World Wars, pneumatics became an obsession for those who predicted an optimistic future of 'instantaneously' inflatable buildings. The wave of enthusiasm culminated in a proliferation of inflatable pavilions at the 1970 Osaka Expo, but the popularity was short-lived. A combination of technical problems, poor workmanship and inadequate design tools led to the technology developing a tarnished image. In spite of all these shortcomings, pneumatic structures have an enduring fascination for biomimics, neatly captured by Reyner Bahnam's assertion that 'inflatables are alive in ways unknown to other building materials'. The first air-filled objects were in all probability inspired by examples in nature such as the function of swim bladders in fish. Stephen Vogel explains the basic principle of pressurised structures in *Cats Paws and Catapults* as follows:

> Making a fluid filled strut is simple. A tension-resisting sheath need only be wrapped around a body of compression-resisting fluid to get a structure that has a discrete shape and an appreciable stiffness, strength and so forth.[22]

This is the basis of much work by the Swiss–Italian engineering firm Airlight Structures, who have developed air beams with impressive spanning capabilities. The beams are reinforced with a steel compression plate on the top, and cable-tension members that run symmetrically from the ends of the plate around each side of the air beam to the middle of the lower face and then up to the far ends of the plate. The essence of their beam design is that the inflated tube both stabilises the compression plate to minimise buckling and creates the structural depth to make it a spanning member. It is exactly equivalent to a conventional steel truss, but neatly avoids the requirement for a substantial top compression member and solid struts. The hard work is done by air at a fairly modest pressure. Doubtlessly there will be scaling limits to the application of this technology but, for the versions that have been tested, it demonstrates a supremely elegant solution that uses a fraction of the materials to achieve the same result. The entry for the Douglas River Bridge (fig. 38) competition by Exploration shows the technology being used to create a super-lightweight span as a link between two areas of valuable biodiversity.

38

38. The Douglas River Bridge by Exploration – using air structurally to create a lightweight crossing

The Inflatable Auditorium

In many ways a temporary auditorium is the perfect brief for pneumatic technology. In theatre design there is a continual quest for spaces that challenge and inspire the artists to create ever more adventurous works. In the Inflatable Auditorium (fig. 39 & 40), designed by Judit Kimpian, the focus was on 'increasing the drama and suspense of a touring event by bringing the building fabric "alive" with . . . asymmetrically curved spaces, transient volumes and dynamic structures'. Other brief requirements that favour inflatables are a desire for rapid deployment with minimum weight and volume while in transit, an aspiration for a high degree of flexibility and, by virtue of its temporary nature, less demanding insulation and thermal-control criteria.

The design developed as a series of wide inflated arch forms that avoided the need for any vertical supports, which always risk obstructing sight lines. The arches connect together to form a stable, although not rigid, structure. Inflatables' strength lies in their ability to transmit loading through deflection – something that characterises many natural structures and a stark contrast with much of the structural engineering of the twentieth century, during which we confused strength with rigidity. In nature, strength is usually achieved not by forming completely rigid structures but by accommodating movement.

The arches of the inflatable auditorium can be moved and their shape modified with pneumatic 'muscles'. The building thus becomes a dramatic spectacle in itself and broadens the range of events that can be accommodated. The bases of the arches move on air castors that double as suction pads similar to those of an octopus so that, once in their new position, they can be secured to the ground with negative pressure. The design also includes inflatable seating and a stage that can expand and contract according to performance requirements. The stage surface is formed from fine metal mesh held in varying degrees of tension by pneumatic muscles. A lighting rig is supported from the inflated arches and stabilised from the ground with reactive pneumatic muscles. While theatres have often been described with mechanistic language, Kimpian shows the potential for theatre as a quasi-living organism that can adapt to a wide range of functions.

Kimpian's work suggests that, with the development of computer software that can accurately model and calculate inflated elements, pneumatic architectural technology has now come of age. Necessary material advances are also within reach, as biomimetic membranes are close to commercialisation. Soap bubbles and cell membranes are able to adapt to minute changes in stress and strain along their surfaces whereas, to date, the membranes that we manufacture are only able to adapt to a very crude extent – by elasticity and local depressurisation. New 'smart' membranes are capable of real controlled shape change, and could transform the performance of pneumatic structures.

The external appearance of the building is distinct from the normal tent form that conventional temporary performance venues normally adopt. Interestingly, concerns about interpretations of biological forms – the directness of which could potentially limit the richness of interpretation – led to an asymmetrical form being adopted. During the short history of inflated structures, some were plagued by forms that were either over-suggestive, grotesque, clichéd or sometimes all three.

Kimpian believes that with design advances in pneumatics, air has been redefined 'not only as a means of support for deployable structures, but as a smart building material which brings the dynamic transformation of space and volume within reach of mainstream architecture', and that 'inflatables can provide a means to realise some of the spatial possibilities emerging from a transient and perpetually evolving digital realm'.

39 + 40

39–40.   Plan and section of the inflatable auditorium by Judit Kimpian
           – 'bringing the building fabric "alive" with asymmetrically
           curved spaces, transient volumes and dynamic structures.'

Deployable structures

Pneumatic technology represents one approach to creating deployable structures, in the way that its products can be rapidly extended through inflation. Such structures have similarities with examples in nature, such as worms and anemones, although the means of extension varies: inflation in the case of pneumatics, the use of muscles in the worm and the pumping of seawater in the anemone.[23] Thomas Heatherwick's Rolling Bridge (fig. 41, 42 & 43) is a good example of a structure that employs methods equivalent to muscles. The bridge is effectively identical to a series of vertebrae with protruding spines that are connected by muscle-like hydraulic rams. By extending or contracting these rams, the bridge can be made to roll up to allow boats through or extend to span over the water for pedestrians.

Another approach to creating deployable structures utilises mechanisms that simply unfold from a compact starting form to an enlarged final shape (fig. 44 & 45). Biological examples of this method that have attracted the attention of biomimetic designers include the hornbeam leaf and the wings of various beetles. Deployables have been of great interest for military and aerospace applications because of the potential they offer for compact transportation and ease of transformation to their fully extended form.

44

45

41–3

One of the pioneers of deployable structures, Chuck Hoberman, certainly appears to have been influenced by biological examples in the design of his Adaptive Shading Esplanade (fig. 46, 47 & 48) project. Similarly, the Al-Husayn Mosque canopies (fig. 49) designed by Bodo Rasch have a striking resemblance to the way that some flowers unfold from their buds. The whole notion of adaptive structures is appealing to a biomimic because it allows buildings to do what most living organisms do – modify their form or behaviour in response to changing conditions. Hoberman has designed many of the most elegant and progressive examples of adaptive, deployable structures, some of which are able to unfold in sections over an atrium roof to provide complete protection from solar gain. It may be that advances in our scientific knowledge of the workings of deployables in nature will lead to further refinements in the form and energy efficiency of human-made structures.

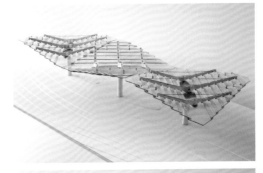

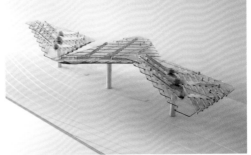

41–3. Hydraulic rams acting as muscles and steel sections as spinal vertebrae in Thomas Heatherwick's 'Rolling Bridge'

44. A deployable structure designed by Guest & Pellegrino (and described in a paper on "Inextensional Wrapping of Flat Membranes") with similarities to certain flowers

45. Convolvulus flower. Some plants have evolved flower petals that can be rapidly deployed from a compact form to fully extended when the conditions are right

46–8. 'Adaptive Shading Esplanade' – one of many adaptive and deployable structures designed by Chuck Hobermann

49. Al-Husayn Mosque canopies designed by Bodo Rasch

46–8

49

Woven, fastened and reciprocating structures

A reciprocating structure is one in which the overall span is longer than that of its individual members and each beam supports, and is supported by, the other beams in the structure.[24] Many bird's nests provide examples of this approach, and it is generally employed when the gap to be spanned – say, between the branches of a tree – exceeds the length of most of the available twigs. Short lengths of stick can be used to successively bridge the distance between two adjacent members that are at an angle to each other, eventually spanning the desired area as a base for the nest. While the nests of some birds are relatively crude accumulations of sticks that rely on gravity and friction to hold them together, other birds use a range of fixing technologies to bind elements together.

The long-tailed tit (*Aegithalos caudatus*) uses a combination of spider silk egg cocoons and fine-leaved mosses as a natural form of Velcro to hold its nest of twigs together.[25] There are numerous examples of adhesives made from bodily secretions, including salivary mucus used by the chimney swift (*Chaetura pelagica*) to make its nests, and the little spiderhunter (*Arachnothera longirostra*) uses pop rivets made of silk to attach its nest to large leaves.[26] The highly sophisticated structures built by the village weaver bird (fig. 50) (*Ploceus cucullatus*) employ as many as six different knots, including loops, half-hitches, hitches, bindings, slip knots and overhand knots, as well as weaving techniques.

There are certainly some elegant examples of human-made structures that use parallel techniques, such as Atelier One's Eton Bridge (fig. 51), the Seiwa Bunraku Puppet Theatre by Kazuhiro Ishii and the Epping Forest

50

51

50. Nest structures built by the village weaver bird using as many as six different knots

51. The Luxmore bridge, Eton College designed by Atelier One and Jamie McColl

52. The Woodland Hall at Epping Forest Burial Park – a timber reciprocating structure (building designer: Graham Brown from 'Out of Nowhere')

52

want to reduce the amount that things move so that people feel safe and less inclined to revisit their lunch. The consequence of this is that the amounts of material used in our structures can look extremely inelegant compared to the more pliant forms found in nature.

Other important distinctions include the fact that we use metals structurally whereas biology does not, and we tend to design for rigidity whereas nature has evolved resilience and toughness. The leg bones of gazelles demonstrate this point. Rather than being straight members, which one might think offered the greatest strength, the bones have a gentle curve. This allows them to absorb much higher shock loading, such as might be experienced when making extreme jumps to escape from a predator. It would perhaps be accurate to categorise the pursuit of rigidity as a twentieth-century aberration, since many vernacular structures deliberately used curved timbers for the same reason as the gazelle – greater resilience.

Burial Park by Graham Brown (fig. 52). However, to the best of my knowledge the direct application of these construction methods from natural structures to human-made ones remains to be explored. Perhaps the most relevant lesson to draw is that nature's woven, fastened and reciprocating structures could provide further clues as to how we can use relatively small structural members to create elegant spanning structures without the need for large primary beams or trusses.

Distinctions between biological and engineered structures

Of course, one of the key differences between biological structures, such as trees, and human-made buildings is that, with the exception of deployables, ours don't move. In fact, most of the time we actively

Conclusions

Many of the examples outlined above demonstrate the potential to achieve radical increases in resource efficiency by using biological structures as a model: manipulations of thin planar surfaces, Nervi's ability to out-compete through lightness, domes and shells achieving factor-10 increases in efficiency and thin pressurised membranes taking this even further to achieve factor-100 increases in resource efficiency. With access to ever-improving scientific knowledge, designers will be able to draw on the many examples of ruthless refinement in nature, as well as the processes that led to that level of refinement, in order to create structures with beauty and efficiency.

In the next chapter, we will see some of the distinctions between our materials and nature's. We will also learn how we might benefit from approximating the molecular-level manufacturing that goes on in nature.

Chapter TWO

How will we manufacture materials?

SPIDERS MAKE THEIR SILK with an array of spinnerets (fig. 53) that produce an aligned stream of polymers which are then 'spun' into a thread with the spider's back legs.[27] When dry, the silk is stronger than Kevlar (aramid, or synthetic polyamide, fibre by another name – the strongest synthetic fibre that we have been able to manufacture to date). The contrast in manufacturing methods is profound. To make aramid fibre requires petroleum to be boiled in sulphuric acid at around 750 °C. The mixture is then subjected to high pressure to get the molecules into place, and the process produces large quantities of toxic waste. So, it takes extremes of temperature and pressure with noxious flows of resources, and yet spiders manage to do the same at ambient temperature and pressure with raw materials of dead flies and water. It does suggest that we still have a lot to learn about manufacturing.

The aramid fibre example is far from exceptional. Our manufacturing methods typically start with energy-intensive mining, crushing, smelting, refining and forming. The process then frequently continues with other stages of treatments, protective coatings and adhesives. Janine Benyus refers to this as a 'heat, beat and treat' mentality, which compares very unfavourably with the manufacturing that goes on in nature.[28] Given our existing challenges of resource depletion, peak oil and climate change, it seems a worthy goal to try to emulate nature's efficiency in our manufacturing processes.

Our use of resources can be characterised as linear, wasteful and polluting, whereas in nature resources are maintained in closed-loop cycles. Our processes regularly produce toxic emissions, which can persist in the environment indefinitely; in the few circumstances in which toxins are used in biology, they biodegrade soon after they have served their specific purposes. The differences in approach and economy become even clearer when one looks at which elements of the periodic table are used in the two approaches. Roughly 96 per cent of all living matter is made from four elements: carbon, oxygen, hydrogen and nitrogen. A further seven elements constitute nearly all of the remaining four per cent: calcium, phosphorous, potassium, sulphur, sodium, chlorine and magnesium. There are then a small number of trace elements that are used in absolutely minute quantities. So, nature uses a very limited subset of the periodic table whereas we use virtually every element in existence, including some that really would be better left in the laboratory.

Professor Julian Vincent has described how, with just proteins and polysaccharides, nature has formed compounds that have all the same properties as human-made ones, stretching from polymers through to high-strength composites.[29] While there are some metals included within the trace elements referred to above (many of which are critical to various biological processes), living organisms do not actually make anything out of metals. Consequently, some might argue that the only truly sustainable materials are ones that can be grown and recycled through biodegradation. For me that is rather an extreme view and just because nature does not make things from, say, aluminium does not mean that we shouldn't.

53. Spinneret glands on the abdomen of a spider from which a fibre is spun tougher than any that humans have made to date. (Image by Dennis Kunkel Microscopy, Inc.)

However, what we can do is to apply some of the principles of resource stewardship found in nature to those metals and minerals that are safe to use. We may also find that there are biomimicry-inspired alternatives for many of the applications for which we currently use metals, and that those alternatives would involve a fraction of the manufacturing energy and environmental impacts.

Cradle to Cradle

Rethinking the whole conundrum of materials and manufacturing is the basis of William McDonough and Michael Braungart's brilliant book *Cradle to Cradle*. In it, they describe the way that most products are manufactured in a 'cradle to grave' manner, such that they have a life of varying length and then the product is disposed of, usually to landfill or by incineration. We do of course recycle a certain amount but many of the things that are made from recyclates are a lower-quality version of the original, and this is what the authors call 'downcycling' – the process by which materials get steadily degraded until they ultimately become waste. Plastics provide a good example in the way that they are often recycled into products like garden furniture but at the expense of material purity. Such products may be made from a mixture of ten or more plastics which are then virtually impossible to separate. Down-cycling therefore just delays the point at which those resources are lost as waste.

Increasingly, manufacturers are trying to make products that are better so they might contain less formaldehyde or have higher recycled content, etc., but *Cradle to Cradle* eloquently describes how being 'less bad' is not the same as being 'good'. At the same time, there are numerous compounds and elements we incorporate into products that are toxic and that persist in the environment – occasionally acting as endocrine disrupters because they are chemically similar to human hormones. European males now have a sperm count that is roughly half that of their grandfathers.[30]

McDonough and Braungart make an important distinction when they describe certain products as 'monstrous hybrids'. These are mixtures of materials or assemblies of components put together in such a way that it is not economically feasible to recycle them and salvage the raw materials after their current lives. Two very common examples from the construction industry are composite floor decks and double-glazed units. In the former, concrete is poured into profiled steel sheets that are so intricately textured that it is unlikely ever to be practicable to separate the two materials; in the latter example, the glass is often given a low-emissivity coating (which would contaminate the glass-production process if recycled) and is then bonded very securely, together with butyl, silicone, aluminium and desiccants – again, confounding economic attempts at recovery of those resources in the future.

McDonough and Braungart ask the questions, 'What about an entirely different model? What would it mean to be 100 per cent good?' They set out to completely eliminate the concept of waste by following the principles of natural systems and keeping all materials in one of two cycles: 'Biological' and 'Technical'. In the biological cycle, which would include natural fibres, wood and so on, all the materials are grown and used in such a way that they can be fully biodegraded at the end of their tenure as a product, reabsorbed into nature and become nutrients for growing other materials. The technical cycle includes all metals and minerals, and the aim with these is that once they have been mined and refined they should remain permanently in the system.

The case studies that McDonough and Braungart describe in their book are drawn mainly from the fields of industrial design and product design. We will now briefly look at how the principles described in *Cradle to Cradle* can be extended to a range of common construction materials and combined with biomimetic solutions.[31]

Solutions in the 'technical cycle'

Graham Dodd from Arup has proposed that one way of creating *Cradle to Cradle* insulated glazed units would be to create spectrally selective glass based on biomimicry. Many colour effects in nature, such as the iridescent wings of the blue *Morpho* butterfly (fig. 54), are achieved not with pigments or coatings but through 'structural colour', which is a microstructure that refracts light rather than reflects it. For glass, it might therefore be possible to create a nanostructure from the glass itself that could perform similarly to the low-emissivity coatings currently applied as a separate material. To avoid other forms of 'monstrous hybridity', it would be necessary to use a thermoplastic seal that is easier to remove and recycle than current examples. The thermal performance of this unit would probably not match conventional ones, but it is important to remember that reducing energy use and related carbon emissions, while extremely important, is not the only challenge we have to address. We may find that quite a few of the most comprehensively sustainable solutions are not necessarily the lowest carbon options.

We may also discover other applications of biological colour creation for products for which we currently use paint coatings. In the metals industry, coatings are inherently problematic because they are almost certain to end up as pollution. Some of the coatings on metals are used for purposes of colouration, but more often they are used to provide weathering protection. Biological materials are able to repair themselves whereas our construction materials are inert and, with a few exceptions discussed later in this chapter, are likely to remain that way for the near future. Consequently, we may see increasing use of metals that are inherently resistant to weathering such as aluminium, stainless steel and Corten steel. There will also be significant advances in technology, such as foamed metals and honeycomb forms, that achieve remarkable increases in resource efficiency.

Concrete can utilise all sorts of by-products from other processes, but cement presents a problem in that it prevents full re-involvement in the technical cycle. Consequently, aggregates become steadily down-cycled.

54.   The irridescent colour of the blue morpho butterfly is the result of a microstructure that creates a colour effect through interference rather than a pigment that reflects particular wavelengths of light

There may be opportunities with geo-polymer cements to create a form of concrete that can be safely reabsorbed into the lithosphere. Similarly, pozzolanic cements and the naturally occurring cementitious compounds that bind together conglomerate rocks could offer good solutions. Concrete is likely to remain a fairly carbon-intensive material, so, when used, we should endeavour to optimise its performance. It can provide very useful thermal mass, and this can be enhanced by articulating the surfaces of soffits and walls. Our lungs are richly articulated to create an effective surface area (fig. 55) for gaseous exchange equal to a tennis court. Adopting a similar strategy for concrete could thermally mobilise a far greater amount of a slab, and deliver more energy savings.

55. Alveoli in an adult human's lung create an effective total surface area roughly equal to that of a tennis court

56. Could the mud-dauber wasp point the way to a lower energy way of compacting materials like rammed earth?

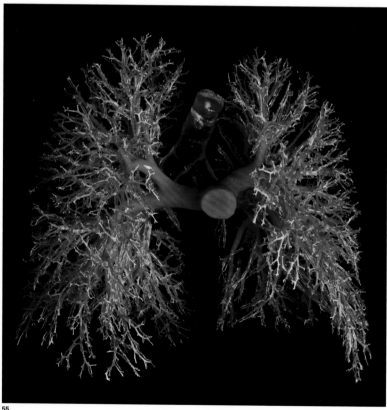

55

Solutions in the biological cycle

Similar challenges regarding coatings apply to timber as they do to metals: most current paint and preservative finishes will invariably end up as pollution. There are a number of revolutionary ways in which we could start to use biological materials, which we will discuss further below, but, in its conventional forms, timber is best selected either for its inherent resistance to weather (woods such as oak, larch and western red cedar) or in the form of products that use non-toxic treatments to extend the wood's life such as ThermoWood® or Accoya®. The first of these uses a short but intense heat treatment to make the wood indigestible to microbes for an extended period, while Accoya® achieves much the same result but through a process of acetylation, using a naturally occurring and benign chemical (acetic acid) that also stabilises moisture content. These options allow the timber to be returned to the biological cycle at the end of its useful life.

Rammed earth has been used as a building material for centuries and has returned to favour owing to its extremely low environmental impact, although it does have serious drawbacks in terms of insulation. Conventionally it is rammed into formwork, either through pure physical labour or assisted by pneumatic compactors. It is worth studying how earth is used by various animal builders who have to make do without power tools. The mud-dauber wasp (fig. 56) (*Trigonopsis*) selects mud for the right consistency and moisture content, holds a pellet against the wall it is building and then turns it into a thixotropic liquid by emitting a buzzing sound. [32] Thixotropy is the property of showing a reduction in viscosity when shaken, and for the wasp it results in very efficient compaction with minimum force. [33] Some animals, notably birds, create a composite material from mud by combining it with plant fibres that give the benefits of strength in tension as well as compression – similar to the function performed by steel rods in reinforced concrete.

Plastics can be made out of plant resins, and if toxic additives or coatings are avoided then the material can be returned to the soil as biological nutrients. However, it should be recognised that currently most crop production involves considerable quantities of oil-based fuels and agrochemicals, so, for the near future at least, it is likely to be better to use oil to make plastics directly or use agricultural residues and then keep the plastics in the technical cycle.

56

Case study
The Plastiki Expedition

The Plastiki Expedition, named after the 1947 Kon-Tiki voyage undertaken by anthropologist Thor Heyerdahl, was initiated by David de Rothschild as a way of drawing attention to the problems of ocean pollution, and focused particularly on the two vast areas of floating waste, located in the gyres formed by ocean currents, known as the Pacific garbage patches. Each of these is the size of Texas and consists mostly of plastic, either in bulk form (which affects seabirds and marine mammals), or as UV-degraded microscopic lengths of polymer which absorb other pollutants and accelerate their uptake into the marine food chain. Those at the top of the food chain are particularly badly affected, including Inuit mothers who are advised not to breastfeed their children because the level of toxins is sufficient for their milk to be classified as hazardous waste.

The garbage patches are a clear example of what is wrong with our current paradigm which involves using resources in a linear, wasteful and polluting way. The brief for the Plastiki was to design a boat made out of plastic bottles, rather than the more common fibreglass, that could be sailed across the Pacific on an expedition that would highlight the problems facing the oceans as well as the kind of solutions that we need to implement. Working with Exploration as concept architects, the team agreed that, to set the right example, the boat should be designed to be fully recyclable at the end of the journey, generate all its own energy and emit no pollution. It was also considered important that the bottles should be used intact rather than simply melted down into a sheet material and turned into a conventional boat.

The first challenge was to find a way to turn a very weak material (plastic bottles) into a structure that would withstand the forces likely to be experienced on a voyage through the Pacific Ocean. The team took inspiration from a number of examples in nature, including pomegranates. This fruit consists of a large number of individual segments packed together in a tight, geometrical way. Any gaps between the segments are filled with pith, and surrounding them all is a tough skin. The end result is a very resilient form, and much of the strength is derived from the internal pressure of each segment against its own membrane. This led to a significant breakthrough in the design process: the idea of pressurising each bottle with air – a simple move that transformed them into incredibly solid objects. Tests proved that, just by adding air pressure, it was possible for two plastic bottles on end to support the weight of a car.

While bundles of bottles provided useful buoyancy, there needed to be a core material to act as a frame for the bottles and to be stiffened by them. The team discovered a sheet material called 'SrPET' (self-reinforced polyethylene terephthalate) that had recently been developed from waste plastic bottles. The revolutionary aspect of this product was that it was made entirely out of one material (PET: polyethylene terephthalate) but in two different forms: a fibre and a matrix. At a molecular level, the fibres are chains of aligned polymers while the matrix is a spaghetti-like tangle of polymers. The structural effect is very similar to the phenomenal toughness of fibreglass; however, unlike fibre glass, which is made using toxic resins and is impossible to recycle, the SrPET can be recycled indefinitely with no loss of resources or material quality – the holy grail of *Cradle to Cradle* design. In fact, the possibility existed to upcycle the bottles and SrPET into products with higher value such as fleece sweaters that could be auctioned off for charity.

Concepts from biomimicry were taken through the whole project, including the design of the cabin by Nathaniel Corum of Architecture for Humanity and the first use of a glue inspired by the adhesive substances secreted by mussels. Consistently with the overall ethos of the project, the energy and waste systems were designed to be zero carbon and to release no emissions to the oceans or atmosphere.

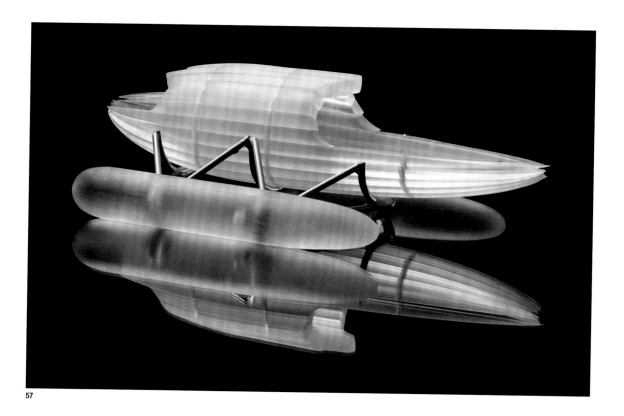

57

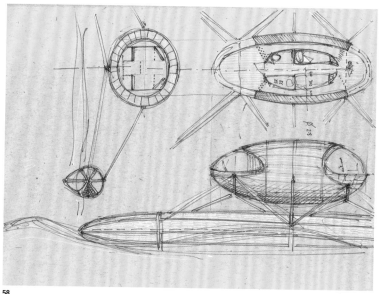

58

57. Early concept model by Exploration for the Plastiki expedition boat

58. Concept sketch of Plastiki expedition boat showing boat hulls made from large bundles of bottles

Can we learn to manufacture in the same way that nature does?

Apart from the differences in the range of elements of the periodic table that are exploited by biology and engineering, there are some other key distinctions that have been usefully summarised by Stephen Vogel and Julian Vincent,[34] as follows:

BIOLOGY	ENGINEERING
Hierarchical structure	Mostly monolithic structure; little or no hierarchy
Interfaces allow separate control of stiffness and fracture	Few interfaces, therefore poor fracture control
Growth by adaptive accretion	Fabrication from powders, melts, solutions
Environmentally influenced self-assembly	Externally imposed form
Environmentally responsive	Very little environmental response
Capable of growth and repair	Obsolescence

In the sections below, we will look at these themes and their implications for mimicking biological manufacturing.

59

Hierarchy and interfaces

Perhaps a good way of exploring the implications of hierarchy would be to consider a range of bridge designs. One means of spanning a modest distance would be to use two solid steel beams that sit on piers at either end. This would represent a monolithic approach with no hierarchy. A more efficient way to span the distance would be to use a pair of steel trusses instead. In a truss, compression members are distinct from tension members and by separating the top compression member from the bottom tension member you can create effective structural depth. That represents one level of hierarchy. Supposing we went one step further so that each compression member in the truss became a small box truss and each tension member became a cable made from stranded steel. That would represent two levels of hierarchy. With increasing levels of hierarchy, the structure becomes more efficient in terms of the amount of material used to achieve a given objective. The Eiffel Tower (fig. 59) demonstrates three levels of hierarchy, but the majority of human engineering uses one level or none at all. In biology, it is not uncommon to find six levels of hierarchy and proportionately higher performance because the structure benefits from bonds at every level from the molecule upwards. The glass sponge *Euplectella* (fig. 60) shows the elegance with which materials can be organised in biology.

You may be feeling confused about the difference between structures and materials, and that is quite justifiable because in biology there really is no distinction between the two. The way that nature makes things from the bottom up, molecule by molecule, means that what we might think of as a biological material is also a structure. Wood (fig. 61), for instance, is a microstructure of lignified cell walls, and bone (fig. 62) is a hierarchical structure of calcium phosphate and collagen molecules in fibrous, laminar, particulate and porous form.

Hierarchical structures also deliver benefits in stiffness and fracture control, and this is achieved through interfaces between, and within, each level of hierarchy. A straightforward example is the abalone

60

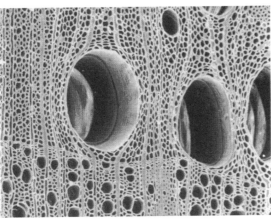

61

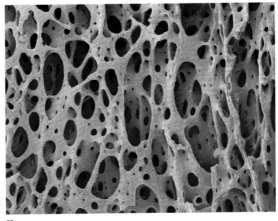

62

59. Trusses within trusses within trusses on the Eiffel tower –
    showing three levels of hierarchy
60. Euplectella, the Venus Flower Basket Glass Sponge – made
    from silica at ambient temperature and pressure with five
    or more levels of hierarchy
61. Scanning electron micrograph showing the microstructure
    of oak (Quercus Robur)
62. Scanning electron micrograph of cancellous (spongey)
    bone tissue

shell which, as we discussed in the previous chapter, is made from platelets of aragonite (a form of calcium carbonate) bonded together with a flexible polymer mortar. In this example the polymer forms the interface, and it is nearly always the case in biology that the material used at these points is weaker than the surrounding substance. As J. E. Gordon explains in his book *The New Science of Strong Materials*, 'This is not because Nature is too incompetent to glue them together properly but because, properly contrived, the weak interfaces strengthen the material and make it tough'.[35] Toughness in engineering terms means resistance to fracture, and although abalone shell is made from the same raw material as chalk, it achieves 3,000 times the toughness through its hierarchical structure and interfaces.

Adaptive accretion and additive manufacturing

The next part of the challenge is the prospect of growing materials for buildings, not in the sense of literal biological growth but by accretion or self-assembly that mimics natural processes. Rapid prototyping was a significant breakthrough for designers in the digital revolution because it allowed a three-dimensional computer model to be turned directly into a physical model with a very high degree of accuracy and without the laborious process of making a prototype by conventional means. Coincidentally, rapid prototyping also approximated the bottom-up manufacturing that goes on in nature in the way that material can be positioned exactly where it needs to be. Consequently, it offered the ability to achieve efficiency of materials through complexity of form. The technology has developed to the point that the hardware is now much cheaper

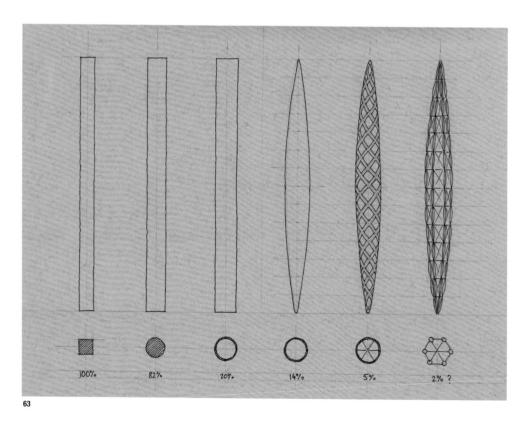

63

and the range of materials that can be used is broad enough to make not just prototype models, but also manufactured elements.

The authority on rapid manufacturing (RM), designer Geoff Hollington, has asserted that this technology now challenges the three traditional ways of making things that have been used since antiquity. The old methods can be summarised as 'subtractive' (such as shaping flint, carving wood or modern machining), 'moulding' (clay pottery, cast metal or moulded plastic) and 'forming' (bending, forging and stamping).[36] New approaches will pioneer 'additive' techniques that approximate the molecular, from-the-bottom-up, manufacturing that occurs in biology. RM machines now exist that allow mixed materials, as nanoparticles in solution, to be deposited from a jet which is similar to that of an inkjet printer. The very small scale of the material allows low-energy bonds such as van de Waal's forces to assist in assembling the particles. If one material that cures to a hard finish is used in combination with another material that dries in a flexible form, then it is possible to produce an element that can be either very tough (exploiting the interfaces), very flexible, or even varying in these properties along its length.

This might give the impression that we have achieved equivalent technology to biological growth processes. We are not quite there yet, but we are getting tantalisingly close. What we ideally want is to be able to use a biological raw material, get it to self-assemble into polymer chains and then be able to assemble those chains in a controlled way.

One of the most promising natural materials is cellulose. It is an underutilised resource from algal biofuel production, and would be easy to extract

because algae do not cross-link the cellulose in their cell walls through lignification. Cellulose is one of the most abundant biological materials and, furthermore, nano-crystals of cellulose can be made to self-assemble into polymer chains.[37] The next critical obstacle to overcome is how to assemble those polymer chains. Essentially, we need an RM 'printer' nozzle that can achieve what the spider spinnerets do, and this is by no means beyond the bounds of possibility. Scientists have succeeded in producing strands of synthesised 'natural' polymers such as silks, collagens and simple spiral forms, albeit not in a rapid and continuous process. The pace of development in RM using metals gives some indication of how the technology will develop. Rapid manufacturing of niche items, such as very small, detailed components and medical implants, is now well-established and is sure to grow to encompass more mainstream applications. Most, if not all, RM is carried out at ambient temperature and pressure and therefore offers the potential for much lower energy fabrication than conventional approaches. The ultimate goal for a biomimic would be to manufacture large structural components from natural polymers such as cellulose or, the even stiffer, chitin (one of the substances from which insect carapaces and crabs shells are made) with many levels of hierarchy for added efficiency and resilience.

Another process that shows some promise is microbial-induced precipitation, which is being researched by Ginger Krieg Dosier at the American

63. Sketch showing how with levels of hierarchy an element of structure can be further refined to use as little as 2% of the material of a solid section

64. Reef, a new wall and ceiling lamp designed by Tanja Soeter for FOC using rapid prototyping / rapid manufacturing methods and giving a sense of the precision with which materials can be manipulated with this technology

64

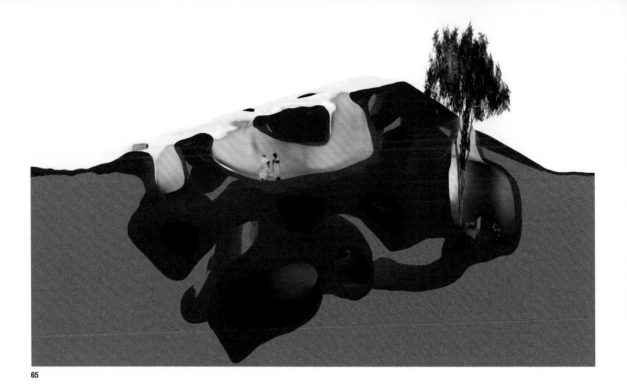

65

University of Sharjah.[38] In this project, layers of sand, calcium chloride and urea are sequentially laid down using an RM machine. Microbial action binds the materials together to form a 'brick' at room temperature, and offers the potential to create masonry blocks without the energy-intensive process of kiln firing. The architect Magnus Larsson has pursued a similar form of microbial precipitation, but with the intention of forming structures *in situ* in desert areas. (fig. 65)

65. Dune – Arenaceous Anti-Desertification Architecture by Magnus Larsson which uses microbial deposition to create habitable structures within sand dunes

66. Pine cones open because the stems of each scale are made from two materials which shrink at different rates when they dry out causing the stems to bend

67. Steffen Reichert and Prof. Achim Menges explored a similar idea to the pine cone in developong a responsive surface made from two veneers. The result is a surface that opens and closes according to changes in humidity and without any sensing or actuation system. (Responsive Surface Structure: Steffen Reichert, Prof. Achim Menges, 2006/07)

Environmental responsiveness

Materials that can sense and respond to changes in their environment are often referred to as 'smart'. Clearly in architecture we create many systems that do this at the level of a building, and it is worth making a distinction here. In most instances of systems engineering, there will be a sensor, a processor and an actuator; in a truly 'smart' material, the sensor and actuator is the same thing and there is no processor.

One example studied by the Centre for Biomimetics at Bath University is the pine cone, which stays firmly closed when it is on the tree. When the cone falls it starts to dry out and open up, eventually releasing the seeds inside. (fig. 66) The opening occurs because the scales of the pine cone have stems made from two materials that react differently to humidity: one of them shrinks more than the other, and the bending effect is similar to that of a bimetallic strip. This idea was developed into a multilayered textile with lots of small flaps that would open up when the wearer started to sweat and close again when the skin beneath has cooled. The concept came to fruition in the form of a tennis top worn by Anna Kournikova.

66

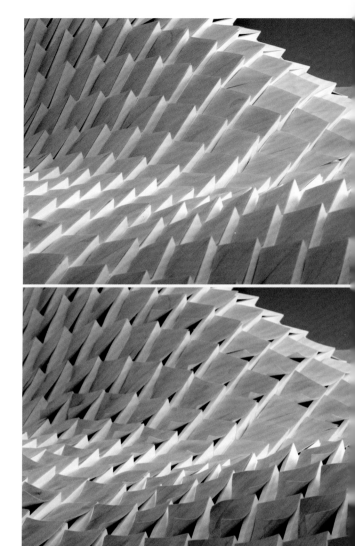

67

A similar idea, also inspired by pine cones, was developed by Achim Menges at the Department for Form Generation and Materialisation at HfG Offenbach, using a composite of veneers (fig. 67) that would either lie flat or roll up according to humidity levels. The potential for façades that can control the internal environment of a building without the need for additional mechanical control is extremely appealing. However, there would be some serious challenges involved in integrating this concept with a building skin that met the many other performance requirements which modern façades must satisfy, such as insulation and air-tightness.

A number of scientists are researching building products inspired by organisms that use bioluminescence. While the intensity of the light given off is generally very low, there is potential for materials that can start to glow at night. There are also products that absorb carbon dioxide from the air, although in a passive rather than smart way. It is highly likely that, in time, many other materials will be developed that can respond to changes in the environment and potentially grow by removing contaminants from the air.

Growth and repair

In building construction, we use a number of materials that have grown, like wood for example, but we do not generally create structures that grow or repair themselves. This is perhaps the area in which there is still the largest gap between biology and engineering, simply because none of our buildings are 'alive' in a sense that is comparable with a living organism. The spider eats its web to recycle it

68

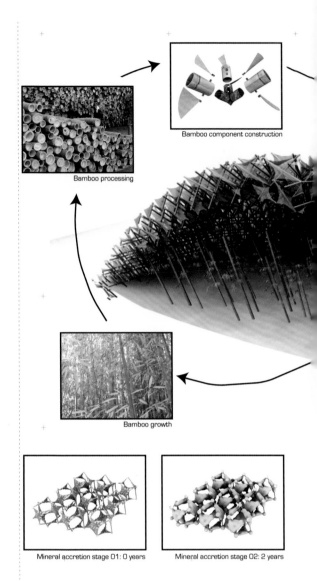

Bamboo processing

Bamboo component construction

Bamboo growth

Mineral accretion stage 01: 0 years

Mineral accretion stage 02: 2 years

when carrying out repairs, and crabs dissolve and reabsorb most of their shells before they shed them in preparation for growing a new one. Our approaches look crude by comparison, and progress on this is only likely to come once we have mastered additive manufacturing with low-energy materials. Then it might be possible for buildings to grow extensions or reinforce themselves in response to environmental demands.

While there are numerous examples of grown structures, such as the living bridges of Cherrapunji, (fig. 68) these would more accurately be referred to as bio-utilisation rather than biomimicry. There are currently very limited instances of growing structures. One of these, 'Biorock™', is discussed below, while another can be found in the work of Rachel Armstrong (Bartlett School of Architecture) and Martin Hanczyc (University of Southern Denmark). They have developed 'protocells', which can be programmed to move away from light and produce a precipitate. A protocell is a small chemical entity that has some of the properties of living cells. One of their proposals is to create protocells that could migrate towards the timber piles that support much of Venice, and reinforce the city's foundations through precipitation of calcium carbonate. A further example of a 'grown' structure can be found in the work of Toby Burgess, who developed a final-year

architectural project for a 'mineral accretion scaffold' which proposes using the evaporation of seawater as a means of building up calcium carbonate on a bamboo framework (fig. 69).

It is easier to find materials with self-repairing qualities. Dr Carolyn Dry (University of Illinois) has developed a form of concrete that has adhesive-filled hollow fibres embedded into the mix, so that if a crack occurs the fibres rupture and adhesive flows into the

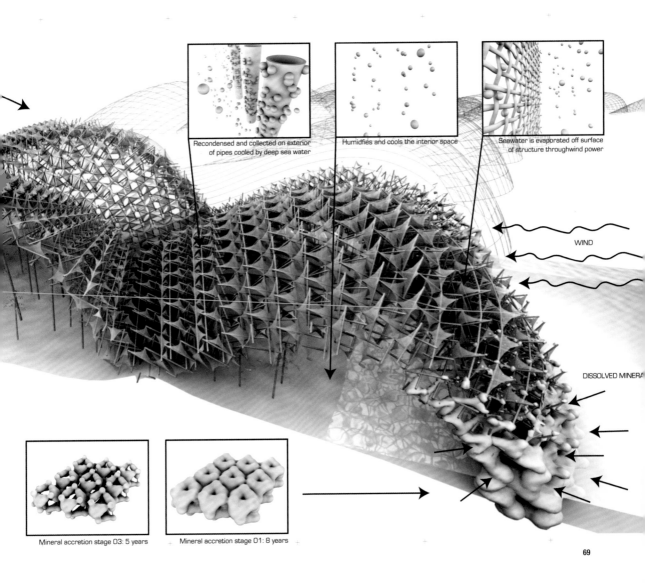

Recondensed and collected on exterior of pipes cooled by deep sea water

Humidfies and cools the interior space

Seawater is evaporated off surface of structure throughwind power

WIND

DISSOLVED MINERA

Mineral accretion stage 03: 5 years

Mineral accretion stage 01: 8 years

69

crack.[39] Dr Henk Jonkers at the Technical University of Delft has created a version of self-repairing 'bio-concrete' that contains limestone-producing bacteria which are activated when a crack occurs.[40] Self-repairing polymers have also been developed, with useful applications in fuel tanks and for other liquids that need safe containment. The clear and strong commercial advantages are likely to draw out further biomimicry-inspired solutions to self repair.

68. The living bridges of Cherrapunji – an example of a grown structure that is still alive

69. Mineral accretion scaffold by Toby Burgess, based on the evaporative deposition of calcium carbonate from seawater

Biorock™

The idea of being able to grow a building to a predetermined form is a compelling one, and Biorock™ (fig. 70) shows some inspiring potential. Pioneered by marine biologist Thomas J. Goreau and engineer / architect Wolf Hilbertz in the 1970s, this technology uses electro-deposition in seawater to form accretive mineral structures. A frame made from steel reinforcing bars is submerged in seawater. An electrical current is then passed through the frame, of a low enough voltage to be safe for marine life but sufficent for dissolved minerals to crystallise out on the structure.

Hilbertz's original plan was to create low-cost structures for developing countries, but when he met Goreau he realised that the idea had great potential to restore coral reefs. The steel frames acquire a coating of mineral within days of being submerged and then form an ideal substrate on which to attach coral species. The corals immediately start to bond and grow. The protection offered by the framework, the presence of the corals and, it is claimed, the low-level electrical field, attract a wide range of other marine life, including fish, crustaceans, octopi and sea urchins. The reefs grow steadily, and in time mature into rich habitats, which, like natural reefs, can provide valuable ecosystem services such as coastal protection.

Biorock™ structures have been built in 15 countries and considerable research has been carried out into their characteristics. The mineral content is determined by the ionic composition of the seawater, and the predominant components are magnesium hydroxide and calcium carbonate. The rate of accretion can be as high as 50 mm per year and, depending on the speed of deposition, the compressive strength varies between 24 and 55 MPa (for comparison, concrete typically has a compressive strength of 17 to 28 MPa while the highest-strength concrete goes up to 80 MPa). The minerals continue to be deposited for as long as the current passes through the frame and damaged areas will repair themselves. Offshore wind turbines or tidal lagoons could use small amounts of surplus electricity to reinforce their foundations with Biorock™, or build reefs that help restore marine ecosystems.

Conclusions
and future challenges

J. E. Gordon, in the second edition of his book *The New Science of Strong Materials*, published in 1976, predicted with great prescience that 'As the subject is developing, it now seems very possible that the coming new engineering materials will resemble much improved versions of wood and bone more closely than they will the metals with which most contemporary engineers are familiar'. The three-and-a-half decades that have elapsed since then have reinforced this view with the new pressures of energy constraints and resource depletion.

The technologies of rapid manufacturing show that there is scope to develop more materials from the biological cycle with the potential for much lower energy processing than the technical cycle. The same energy- and resource-depletion pressures will drive our use of materials from the technical cycle towards models of cyclical stewardship that mimic natural systems. It is readily conceivable that making construction elements using cellulose in rapid manufacturing could achieve factor-100 savings in energy compared to conventional approaches.[41]

The shift from a linear, wasteful and polluting way of using resources to a closed-loop model is one of the essential transformations that we will need to undergo to arrive at truly sustainable architecture. Notions of closed-loop stewardship of resources and biomimetic manufacturing are inextricably linked, as Julian Vincent has neatly summarised:

> Our materials are rendered biologically inert through the introduction of high energy bonds (necessarily using high temperatures). Biological materials have evolved to be recycled, and their molecules are stabilised by bonds that are only just strong enough for the expected conditions of temperature and mechanical function.[42]

This leads us to the next subject area: systems thinking, and how we can rethink human-made systems to mimic the remarkable efficiencies of ecosystems.

70. A 'Biorock' structure grown in seawater through electro-deposition of minerals and, in this case, used as a substrate for coral reef restoration

Chapter THREE

How will we create zero-waste systems?

THE WHOLE SUBJECT of waste is characterised by contradictions. It is extremely unglamorous and yet offers huge potential; it is largely ignored by designers and yet the few projects that explore this area demonstrate wonderful ingenuity; it is based on the use of the word 'waste' that is by one reading dismissive (worthless material), and by another interpretation revealing of its possibility (a lost opportunity). This chapter will describe how natural systems operate and what we can learn from them in order to rethink our own systems. The prospect exists of deriving far more value from the same resources while moving towards zero-waste ways of operating. As mentioned in the introduction to this book, this shift from a linear, wasteful and polluting way of using resources to a closed-loop model is one of the most important transformations that we need to bring about.

While we are not going to dwell on the problems, it is worth at least identifying some of the key issues. The sewage-disposal system devised by Joseph Bazalgette in 1859 was in many ways a huge breakthrough in public health and sanitation. However, some of his critics at the time correctly predicted what would later become the biggest loss of nutrients in the history of civilisation. Bazalgette's contemporary, Justus von Liebig, had studied the Roman sewers and the efficiency with which they had transferred vast quantities of

minerals from the soils, via the collective digestive system of the Roman Empire, out into the Mediterranean. Liebig urged the British Prime Minister of the time to adopt a system that returned the nutrients to the fields of Britain and, in what may prove to be his most prescient remark, observed that 'The equilibrium in the fertility of the soils is destroyed by this incessant removal of phosphates'.[43] Amory Lovins describes how in the US the quantity of materials per person mobilised into the economy every day is 20 times the average citizen's body weight and, of that, only one per cent is still in use six months later.[44] From one perspective this appears ridiculous or even tragic (if you want to be melodramatic about things), but from an ecosystems view it represents an enormous opportunity to create more value out of the same resources while moving towards zero waste. One of the most important lessons to be learned from biological systems is that of seeing waste as an opportunity.

Ecosystems

Most of us will remember the diagrams from our biology and geography classes that showed the carbon, nitrogen and hydrological cycles. Plants, through photosynthesis turn atmospheric carbon dioxide into sugars and, with the addition of other elements taken up through their roots, are able to grow and form the basis of most food webs. Nitrogen is fixed into the soils by particular plants that have evolved a symbiotic relationship with bacteria called *Rhizobium*. When plants

71.   The renowned mycologist Paul Stamets has
      described fungi as 'the grand molecular
      disassemblers of nature'

die, drop leaves or are digested and excreted by animals and microorganisms, the carbon, nitrogen and other elements are returned to the soil. Water, the universal solvent for nearly all biological reactions, is also cycled through ecosystems and ultimately evaporated into the air to be returned as rainfall.

It is also worth remembering how ecosystems start and become established. A bare surface of rock gets eroded by wind, ice and rain, and the grit from this process, rich in minerals, gathers in hollows and crevices. Lichens and other species assist in extracting nutrients from the rock and contribute to the formation of simple soils. Mosses and grasses can then get established. Over time, humus accumulates and the diversity of microorganisms in the soil expands. Eventually, larger plants such as the mountain ash, which also happens to be a nitrogen fixer, are able to grow and continue the enrichment of the soil.

While this is an example of relatively slow ecological succession, the process can occur much more quickly if, for instance, there is a landslide that reveals a large area of bare earth. Some pioneer species arrive very quickly and change the environment slightly such that other plants, a whole range of competing primary colonisers, can establish themselves. They in turn make it possible for secondary colonisers to grow and at the same time they create niches for other organisms. Below the ground is another world entirely of worms, insects, fungi and microorganisms. The process of succession continues until it reaches a 'climax ecosystem', which in most parts of the UK would be oak woodland. So, at what stage is the level of biodiversity the greatest? It might be tempting to think that it is somewhere in the middle of this process when there are a large number of species competing for dominance. However, the diversity of the system continues to increase all the way through to the climax ecosystem, and the reason for this is that, all the time, the number of ecological niches is increasing and making it possible for growing numbers of interdependent species to become established. Janine Benyus neatly summarises this characteristic of ecosystems by saying that 'life creates conditions conducive to life'[45] – the more that ecosystems mature, the more they enhance their environment and allow for greater diversity.

At this stage, it would be worth summarising some of the differences between biological systems and the kind of human systems that the current paradigm creates:[46]

BIOLOGICAL SYSTEMS	HUMAN-MADE SYSTEMS
Complex	Simple
Closed-loop flows of resources	Linear flows of resources
Densely interconnected and symbiotic	Disconnected and mono-functional
Adapted to constant change	Resistant to change
Zero waste[47]	Wasteful
No long-term toxins used	Long-term toxins frequently used
Distributed and diverse	Often centralised and mono-cultural
Run on current solar 'income'	Fossil-fuel dependent
Optimised as a whole system	Engineered to maximise one goal
Regenerative	Extractive
Use local resources	Use global resources

Clearly there are exceptions to these, but the general characteristics hold true in many cases and often the distinctions become more marked as human-made systems mature. In biological cases, there are millions of contributors to the system, no unemployment and numerous opportunities for nature's equivalent of entrepreneurship – species that evolve into a wide variety of ecological niches. In human-made systems, large multinationals often dominate, power resides with a few individuals, a degree of unemployment is deemed necessary and creative entrepreneurship is limited.

Mimicking ecosystems

A number of organisations have created industrial networks that mimic natural systems and, by doing so, radically increase the amount of useful outputs from the same inputs. Early examples – such as Kalundborg, an industrial complex in Denmark involving the co-location of a power plant, chemical works and other processes – have been superseded by schemes in which all the core elements are compatible with natural systems.

The civil engineer George Chan pioneered an eco-systems approach in the development of a sorghum brewery in Tsumeb, Namibia, which promised to deliver 'Good beer, no pollution, more sales, and more jobs'.[48] Breweries conventionally use large quantities of water and grains, of which only a fraction remains in the finished product. Often the alkaline waste water, which contains low levels of biological contamination, undergoes expensive chemical treatment before disposal and the spent grains are given away as cattle feed. The latter outcome is far from ideal because the grains are too fibrous and this results in the cattle producing more methane, which is one of the most potent greenhouse gases. Chan approached both of these problems as opportunities for adding elements to the system that created more value from exactly the same inputs.

Chan's solution was that the waste water would be used for cultivating the alga *Spirulina*, rich in protein and micronutrients and therefore effective at combating malnutrition. After this process, the water was used for fish farming to produce further sources of protein. Through the creation of large water bodies with a diversity of aquatic life, the normal processes of evaporation and infiltration ensured that the water cycle was closed and that the secondary benefits of recharging groundwater were achieved. The spent grains were an ideal substrate for growing mushrooms, as up to one tonne of fungi can be produced from four tonnes of grain.[49] After mushroom cultivation, the substrate, rich in fungal mycelium is then more suitable for animal feed or earthworm composting. The earthworms were used to feed chickens and the manure went to an anaerobic digester, which produced gas for the brewery and the local people to reduce demand for wood.

The end result was a system that produced 12 products instead of just one; seven times as much food, fuel and fertiliser; four times as many jobs as a conventional approach and a fraction of the waste.[50] Gunter Pauli, founder of the Zero Emissions Research Initiative (ZERI), and an enthusiast for industries modelled on ecosystems, summarises the benefits of this approach as follows:

> Remarkable solutions emerge from reinterpreting the nature and function of energy and nutrients, allowing us to achieve greater resource efficiency, to build competitive industries, and to adopt innovations that generate jobs and create added value. This is how ecosystems evolve to ever more efficient systems, requiring ever less energy expenditure for ever more species.[51]

The Cardboard to Caviar Project

The Cardboard to Caviar Project (also known as the 'ABLE Project') is an inspired example of how linear, wasteful arrangements can be transformed into closed-loop systems that produce no waste and yield much greater productivity. Conceived by Graham Wiles of the Green Business Network (GBN) in Kirklees and Calderdale, northern England, the scheme started as a way of involving people with disabilities in a recycling initiative. Waste cardboard was collected from shops and restaurants, and was shredded so that it could be sold to equestrian centres as horse bedding. The second stage was to compost the used bedding through vermiculture, and initially the idea was to sell the surplus worms to a fishing-bait supplier. At the eleventh hour the supplier backed out, so Graham Wiles, not being the kind of person that gives up easily, decided to cut out the middleman and set up his own fish farm.

Working now with reforming heroin addicts, a fish farm was established to raise Siberian sturgeon. Wiles noticed that many of the youngsters were coming to the site each day with junk food, so he decided to involve them in growing vegetables and learning about healthier eating. Allotments were created nearby, and vegetable waste was used to supplement the worms and reduce dependence on commercial fish food which is generally made from fishmeal. It became clear that the rate of fish growth slowed during winter because the water was too cold. By this stage, Yorkshire Water, who ran the adjacent sewage works agreed to give a further 10 hectares of former industrial land to the project as well as treated-sewage pellet fertiliser. The team set about planting short-rotation willow to feed a biomass boiler.

One of the supervisors on the project had experience of fish farming in developing countries, and redesigned the proprietary filtration system using reclaimed water-storage tanks. The filtered water still had high levels of nitrates and phosphates, so this was fed into linear tanks planted with watercress. The plants absorbed most of the nutrients while creating another food product that could be continuously cropped, as well as clean water to feed back into the fish tanks. The sludge from the new system was fed into worm composting beds, and some was put into buckets of water to attract mosquitoes in order to create a regular supply of larvae for the fish hatchlings.

Food production was extended by planting a large area of the available land with fruit trees. Clover provided ground cover, nitrogen fixation for the soil and pollen for a thriving colony of bees in 21 hives. The site has been transformed from a degraded industrial plot into a haven for biodiversity. The scheme has been extremely successful in getting addicts off drugs and into more constructive pursuits. Whereas the local authority rehabilitation programmes were often costing £100,000 per addict per year (not counting other costs, such as crime and policing) and experiencing a 95 per cent failure rate, the Able Project has had an 80 per cent success rate. When visiting the project, it is easy to see why: the calming sound of the water and the nurturing of fish creates a sense of responsibility, and the way in which the project is both restorative and inclusive in activities that deliver tangible results all contribute to its rehabilitative effect. The production of caviar demonstrates the potential to turn a waste material into a high-value product while yielding social, economic and environmental benefits. The caviar could be sold back to the restaurants that supplied the cardboard, to close a particularly satisfying and alchemical loop.

The project continues to evolve. New types of fish, tilapia and carp, are being raised to supply anticipated demand from local southeast-Asian and Polish communities. A maggot farm using another waste stream, mouldy bread (which produces none of the smells of meat-based production), is being set up to enrich the fishes' diet and eliminate the need for any supplementary fish food to be bought in. A fish smoker is also to be built in order to create higher-value products, and this time Wiles is keen to work with ex-service personnel. Soldiers often return from conflict zones with severe disabilities and post-traumatic stress disorder and find it very difficult to fit into civilian life, which frequently leads to homelessness and crime.

If we refer to the list above that compared biological with human-made systems, we can see that the Able Project fits very clearly into the left-hand column. It has developed into a complex system of interdependent activities, and there is a sense in which, just as with ecological succession, the more the project grows the more the possibilities expand. It has transformed a number of waste streams into valuable products and re-engaged what is arguably the most deplorable form of waste – underutilised human resources with great skills to offer and a desire to be involved.

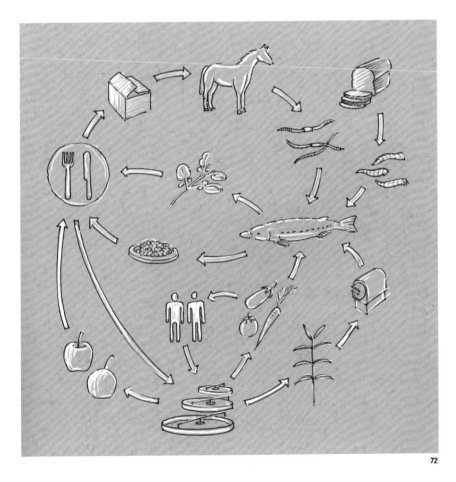

72

72.   Diagram showing the diverse and growing
      elements of the Cardboard to Caviar project

How are ecosystems thinking and architecture connected?

No doubt some readers will now be thinking 'Hang on. I'm an architect not a farmer. This is ridiculous'. Well, feel free to skip to the next chapter but you'll be missing out on some important innovations in urban planning and ways in which buildings can be integrated into resilient, enriching contexts. Let's look at some of the arguments for pursuing ecosystems thinking in a bit more detail.

Many of the best examples of mimicking ecosystems are indeed based on food production rather than processing building materials, but that boundary exists mainly because of the challenge we identified at the end of the last chapter. Generally we manufacture materials with high energy bonds, which makes them difficult to integrate into systems modelled on biology. If buildings, cities and products were made from stuff like natural polymers, with low energy bonds, then there could be a perfect fit and we would see more building materials featured in these cycles. This shift is already underway.

Models based on ecosystems involve complex interactions between different processes that require design input if they are to be optimised. New building types will emerge from the transition to a zero-waste society, and the potential exists to celebrate these as great works of architecture.

Conventionally built structures have tended to draw down on natural capital and degrade their context, whereas ecosystems thinking is an opportunity to do the opposite. Carolyn Steel articulates clearly in *Hungry City* the way that food used to be something that richly animated public spaces in towns and cities.[52] As an urbanised society, we have become increasingly disconnected from food. Creating interconnected systems of growing food, producing building materials and dealing creatively with waste would re-establish a connection with food while creating resilient and vibrant places to live.

Designing a sustainable built environment is not just about architecture, it's also about strategic planning and infrastructure that embraces food, transport and energy as well as health and well-being. One of the champions of this idea is Pooran Desai of Bioregional, who makes the point in *One Planet Communities* that ecosystems thinking can help to make the shift from an economic model in which 'resources, energy and capital investments flow through the economy, becoming waste, to closed loop processes where wastes become inputs for new processes'.[53] Economists such as E. F. Schumacher and Richard Douthwaite have argued convincingly for the benefits of local economic development and the 'multiplier effect' of money being spent numerous times before it leaves the local economy. The UK Sustainable Development Commission estimates that for each £10 spent on local organic food, £25 of value is created in the local economy, whereas the same £10 spent in a supermarket generates only £14 of value.

The more critical reader might also be wondering whether the new models we have discussed in this chapter are really biomimicry or bio-utilisation. The answer is both. Many of the individual elements in these systems would best be described by the latter term, in that they directly implement a biological process for human benefit. However, the way that these are deliberately brought together in synergistic systems is very definitely biomimetic, and a critical part of a restorative approach.

Using what is abundant

Another characteristic of biological organisms is that they use what is abundant. Nature is a great opportunist, and if at any point there is an unexploited resource in an ecosystem then an organism will arrive to occupy that niche or, in the longer term, evolve to take advantage of the opportunity presented. There are interesting parallels here with architects that work with found materials – often waste materials or resources that exist on a site. The architects and students at the Rural Studio in Hale County, Alabama, have created some exceptional buildings using waste resources with great ingenuity. Carpet tiles, vehicle-licence plates (fig. 73), truck windscreens and a whole range of other locally available resources have been transformed into architecture for poor communities in Alabama. Biological organisms

73

rarely bring building materials over long distances to the site; instead they bring evolved ingenuity to the site and create structures with what exists there.

There are sensible limitations to the idea of local sourcing for architecture. Some parts of modern low-energy buildings inevitably need to be high-performance elements manufactured under carefully controlled conditions. Local sourcing is best pursued

73. During the course of evolution organisms have evolved to make use of what is abundant and we could gain a lot from developing our ingenuity with under-utilised resources in an equivalent way. The architects at Rural Studio have designed some of the best examples of this approach – sometimes using vehicle windshields, carpet tiles or, in this case, license plates as shingles

for heavy, bulky materials that would otherwise be energy intensive to transport to the site, or for waste materials that can be transformed in some way.

The idea of using what is locally abundant informed the design process for Grimshaw's Eco Rainforest, (fig. 74) which was conceived for a site that was being operated as a landfill facility with another few years to run. While the brief for a large Eden-like botanical visitor attraction did not require any interaction with the waste-handling aspects of the site, the team decided that the design should engage with the subject of resource flows in some way. Inspiration came from two main sources: the Cardboard to Caviar Project and the pineapple sheds at Heligan Gardens in Cornwall. The latter were built in the Victorian era as a way of growing the highly fashionable pineapple in the cold and damp British climate. South-facing stepped planting beds were arranged under glass, and fresh manure mixed with straw was loaded into large cavities in the walls. The heat from the decomposition process was enough to raise the air temperature around the pineapple plants to 25 °C, which maintained growth throughout the winter. For the Eco Rainforest, the architects conceived of the building as something that could be entirely built from, and run on, recycled resources.

In many ways simply an enlarged version of the pineapple sheds, the scheme comprised a south-facing glass roof supported on massive walls made from masonry rubble loaded into gabion wire baskets. Within the walls, large vertical bio-digesters were incorporated that could process biodegradable waste from the cities nearby. For much of the year the building would be self heating, just using passive solar gain and the thermal mass in the walls. During colder times of the year, heat pumps would allow warmth from the decomposition process in the bio-digesters to be drawn off in order to heat the botanical enclosure.

It was proposed early on in the design process that the scheme should have an educational focus on ecosystems, and that notionally the exhibited plants and animals should aim to recreate a piece of Amazonian rainforest as faithfully as possible. As the design progressed and various innovative approaches to closed-loop resource use were proposed for the site, it

74

became clear that there could be a clear link between the exhibit and the way that the scheme would operate similarly to an ecosystem. While the project did not proceed to construction, an economic analysis of the landfill-tax credits, and the value of the heat, compost and electricity generated from gasified green waste suggested that the scheme could generate as much as £9 million per year. By using what was abundant, the project proposed a way in which a huge problem, landfill, could be turned into a massive opportunity with multiple benefits.

74. The Eco-Rainforest by Grimshaw – a scheme that was to be almost entirely built from, and run on, waste resources

75. De Kas – A restaurant set up inside a productive greenhouse by Gert Jan Hageman

Case study
The Mobius Project

While in the twentieth century we became accustomed to separating activities into large-scale mono-functional operations, the Mobius Project by Exploration brings together a whole range of productive processes in a way that allows inputs and outputs to be connected up to form a closed-loop model. The scheme incorporates the following elements:

- A productive greenhouse, including community allotments growing a range of crops that would not flourish outdoors
- A restaurant serving seasonal food grown inside and locally to the greenhouse
- A fish farm rearing a range of edible fish
- A food market
- A wormery composting system
- Mushroom cultivation using waste coffee grains
- An anaerobic digester and biomass CHP
- A 'Living Machine'[54] water-treatment system, as pioneered by John Todd
- Artificial limestone formation from waste CO_2, using accelerated carbonation technology[55]

There are three main cycles: food production, energy generation and water treatment. Many of the individual components of the scheme have been explored previously. In Amsterdam, a highly successful restaurant called De Kas (fig. 75) was established by Gert Jan Hageman in a greenhouse that was due to be demolished. Since its opening in 2001, it has continued to serve 50,000 visitors every year with food, from the greenhouses, virtually unparalleled in its freshness. The Able Project and Eco Rainforest have shown the potential for creating productive food systems on waste streams, and John Todd's work has shown how grey and black water from urban areas can be treated using plants and microorganisms. Similarly, mushrooms cultivated in coffee waste, anaerobic digestion and accelerated carbonation have all been developed and implemented on varying scales.

The innovative aspect of the Mobius Project (fig. 76) is in the way that it co-locates and integrates these processes in synergistic cycles. The building can handle much of the biodegradable waste from a local urban area using composting and anaerobic digestion. The methane derived from this process can be used to generate electricity and heat for the greenhouse, while some of the flue gases can be captured by accelerated carbonation and turned into building materials. The restaurant, apart from being supplied with fruit, vegetables and fish from the greenhouse, which cuts down on food miles, can operate at close to zero waste as food waste can be fed to fish or composted. Solids from waste water can be diverted to the anaerobic digesters, while the remaining water can be treated for reuse. Fertiliser from the various forms of waste handling can be used in the greenhouse, and the significant surplus can help to remediate brownfield land on the outskirts of the city.

75

The scheme could play an important role in generating a sense of community and reconnecting people with food while addressing many of the infrastructural requirements of sustainable living in urban areas. The idea of reconnecting activities that are currently centralised and disconnected offers the potential to achieve what biological systems do – transforming waste into nutrients. These benefits however, need to be tempered with realism as many of the individual elements will have minimum scales of economic viability and certain functional constraints.[56] At the same time, we need to be conscious of factors that are normally excluded from economic calculations as 'externalities', such as pollution, nutrient loss and urban deprivation. Working out the 'right' solution for any given location involves a more complicated analysis than that which conventional economics generally delivers.

In *The Omnivore's Dilemma*, the food writer Michael Pollan describes the way in which raising cattle in feedlots produced health and waste problems that did not occur when the cattle were raised on grass. It was, he said, a way of 'turning one elegant solution into two intractable problems'.[57] The potential exists with schemes like the Mobius Project to reverse this flawed paradigm – to transform the whole metabolism of our cities and convert our problematic, linear systems into closed-loop solutions while addressing the food, energy, water and waste challenges of sustainable urbanism.

Conclusions on waste and ecosystems thinking

If waste is seen as a nutrient or an underutilised resource, then a new economic paradigm emerges and wealth can be created by consuming fewer resources.

What is clear from even a cursory look at our conventional industrial, agricultural and urban systems is that the way resources flow through our economies represents a huge opportunity. The brewery example revealed that only a few per cent of the resources made their way into the finished product, while Gunter Pauli has described even more extreme examples, such as coffee production which gives 'value to only 0.2% of the biomass while the rest is left to rot'.[58] If we contemplate that in many cases the unused portion of those resources will have been expensive disposal problems, which are likely to become even more costly in the future, then the potential offered by ecosystems thinking becomes even more pronounced.

While the evolution of ecosystems has rewarded nature's equivalent of entrepreneurs (the organisms that have evolved to fill new ecological niches), the same opportunities exist in human-made versions of ecosystems: rewarding those that can turn waste into value and jobs. Some of the examples may seem quirky, such as turning cardboard into caviar, but their significance should not be underestimated. Traditional economics is based on liquidating natural capital into financial and physical capital, often at the expense of social capital. This made a certain sense at the start of the Industrial Revolution when resources were abundant and people were scarce, but in the twenty-first century the opposite scenario is developing. The importance of natural capital is increasingly apparent, as is the need to provide livelihoods for a growing number of people. Many of the examples based on ecosystem thinking reflect exactly those values, being restorative to the immediate environment and helping to build local resilience through re-engaging marginalised groups of people.

There will be an urgent need in the future for designers to work more closely with industrialists and biologists to create forms of industrial symbiosis that are integrated into mixed-use communities with the benefits that arise from combining residential and employment areas. Instead of the inherent risk involved in basing communities around mono-functional industries, models based on ecosystems thinking would involve a diversity of functions.[59]

76. The Mobius Project by Exploration with Yaniv Peer and Filippo Privitali. A scheme that brings together a number of activities in synergistic cycles

Chapter FOUR

How will we manage water?

WATER IS BECOMING an increasingly contentious topic, both environmentally and politically. The consensus amongst climate scientists predicts that much of the developing world in tropical latitudes will experience a substantial loss of agricultural productivity owing to temperature increases and a reduction in rainfall. Other parts of the world, generally temperate regions, are likely to experience increased precipitation, both in terms of quantity and intensity, which, unless managed, will increase the risk of flooding.

Until now, we have managed to feed the world's growing population in large part owing to the achievements of the so-called 'green revolution' in high-yielding seed varieties pioneered by the agronomist Norman Borlaug. The increases in crop yields achieved from these technological advances were impressive, but they are looking increasingly fragile because they are dependent on large quantities of fertiliser and irrigation. Most synthetic fertilisers are fossil-fuel intensive in their production and, if peak oil theories prove to be correct, oil prices will increase substantially in the coming decades.[60] Irrigation water is very often extracted from aquifers at such a rate that the water is likely to turn saline as it becomes recharged with seawater. Recent history has shown that there is a very direct link between water shortages and armed conflict. Even a ten-year extrapolation of existing trends in climate change, water supplies and population growth raises some alarming possibilities.

All the issues described above present significant challenges for designers. The good news is that many comparable problems have already been solved by organisms that have had to adapt to environments in which water is scarce, intermittent or overabundant. Some species have evolved ways of harvesting water from the air in deserts, others store water for periods of scarcity or thrive in locations with as much as 11 m of rainfall per annum. This chapter will explore some of these examples and show how biomimicry could help deliver radical increases in water efficiency.

Minimising water loss

All creatures adapted to living in arid conditions have some means of reducing water loss. This often involves using non-living matter to create shade, trapping a layer of air next to the organism's surface to reduce the evaporative gradient or a combination of the two. Some birds that live in deserts have black plumage, which might seem like a bizarre strategy but the feathers are simply protein structures (made from non-living keratin), which, through their opacity, prevent most of the sun's heat reaching the bird's skin and consequently reduce water loss. Numerous species of cacti are covered in fine, white filaments, which not only reflect the sun but also help to trap humid air next to the living tissue so that the exchange of gases necessary for photosynthesis can continue while water loss

77. Centre-pivot irrigation fields. In many parts of the world ground water is being extracted at such a high rate that the aquifers are becoming recharged with salt water with devastating implications for the agriculture on which people depend

is minimised. The umbrella thorn tree (*Acacia totilis*) retains large amounts of dead branches, which appear to serve no function other than to provide shade for the living tissue and for the soil beneath so that evaporation is reduced.

Similar strategies could be used more extensively for buildings in hot climates: opaque or reflective structures, for example, that provide shade and could, as we will see below, double as water collectors. Increasing shade around such schemes could also help to hold a layer of cooler air at ground level and provide comfortable conditions for people while reducing evaporation from the soil.

Water storage

Some habitats are characterised by intermittent rainfall, with, in extreme cases, the whole year's meagre precipitation falling in a few hours. This goes a long way towards explaining why cacti often have ribbed stems like concertinas (fig. 78). These structures can absorb large quantities of water very quickly without any significant new growth – simply by expansion.

Other plants have adapted to intermittency by storing their water below ground in large, swollen roots. Perhaps the most extreme example of this is the elephant foot – a species of yam which can grow tubers that weigh as much as 300 kilogrammes. What does this suggest for architecture? Water storage in buildings is almost without exception in the form of rigid tanks, often built underground with considerable cost and embodied carbon. There could be potential for expandable storage vessels made from lightweight membranes to be incorporated into walls or landscape features. This would allow buildings to harvest a far larger proportion of the rain that falls during the infrequent rainstorms that characterise some arid climates. Such a strategy could make sense for remote sites that would otherwise require expensive infrastructure to connect to mains water. The chances of flash flooding caused by roof-rainwater discharge would also be reduced.

79

Water harvesting

It would be hard to find a better example of what biomimicry can offer than the Namibian fog-basking beetle (fig. 79). This creature has evolved a way of harvesting its own fresh water in a desert. The way it does this is by climbing, at night, to the top of a sand dune and, because it is matt black, radiating heat to the night sky and become slightly cooler than its surroundings. When the moist breeze blows in off the sea, droplets of water form on the beetle's back. Then, just before sunrise, it tips its shell up, the water runs down to its mouth, it has a good drink and goes off and hides for the rest of the day. The effectiveness of this beetle's adaptation goes even further, because it has a series of bumps on its shell which are hydrophilic and between them is a waxy finish which is hydrophobic. The effect of this is that as the droplets form on the bumps they stay in tight spherical form, which means that they are much more mobile than they would be if it was just a film of water over the whole beetle's shell. So, even when there is only a small amount of moisture in the air,

the creature is still able to harvest it effectively. It's a remarkable adaptation to a resource-constrained environment, and consequently very relevant to the kind of challenges we are going to be facing over the next few decades.

This amazing insect has inspired numerous schemes, including the Seawater Greenhouse, the Las Palmas Water Theatre and, as we shall see in the final chapter, the Sahara Forest Project. All of these projects apply the same idea to create an equivalent water-harvesting technology. The fog-basking beetle has been studied in detail by biologist Andrew Parker, who has since worked with the firm QinetiQ to produce a type of plastic with the same combination of hydrophilic and hydrophobic surfaces to enhance condensation.

78. The ribbed forms of cacti allow them to quickly expand to absorb water when there is rainfall

79. The Namibian fog-basking beetle – a biomimicry hero

80 + 81

The Seawater Greenhouse (fig. 80 & 81) is an invention designed by Charlie Paton that uses the evaporation of seawater at the front of the enclosure to create a cool and humid growing environment for crops in arid regions. The plants inside benefit from lower temperatures, and the high humidity results in much lower transpiration rates so that irrigation requirements are reduced by as much as a factor of eight. The flow of air is largely wind driven and at the back of the greenhouse a second evaporator, supplied with hot seawater from black pipes in the roof, raises the temperature and absolute humidity of the air at this point. This hot, saturated air then passes a series of vertical polythene pipes which are supplied with cool seawater from the bottom of the front evaporators. The polythene pipes are equivalent to a large area of beetle's shell, and form a condensation surface for the humidity. Droplets of water form on the surface of the pipes and run down to a tank to supply the irrigation water needed for the crops. The building essentially mimics and enhances the conditions in which the beetle harvests water: evaporation of seawater is increased to create higher humidity, and then a large surface area is created for condensation. Saline water is turned into fresh water just using the sun, the wind and a small amount of pumping energy. Incidentally, there are some biological examples of direct desalination, such as penguins and mangrove trees, which could inspire other approaches, although these are more likely to lead to improvements in membrane-based desalination rather than being powerful generators of architectural form.

There are numerous other examples of plants that recover water from humid air simply by creating a large surface area of leaves on which thick fog can condense. A species of laurel (*Ocotea foetens*) that grows on El Hierro in the Canary Islands does this to such an effective degree that one particular specimen achieved sacred status. According to legend, during the sixteenth century a mature example, known as the Garoé laurel tree or the fountain tree, provided enough water to supply the local population during periods of siege. This process can be readily mimicked by erecting fog nets, as Dr Robert Schemenauer has done on other parts of the Canary Islands that were denuded of vegetation during the twentieth century. The nets capture droplets of water, which are funnelled down to a sapling at the base. Once the sapling has grown to a certain size it is able to capture its own moisture from the fog, which tends to linger a few metres above the ground because the earth stays relatively warmer than the air. In locations that experience mist on a regular basis, the same trick could be applied to buildings – designing cladding that mimicked the leaves of the laurel and perhaps harvested all the water needed for the occupants.

Camels have highly intricate nasal structures, known as turbinates, which are made from spongy bone covered with richly vascular tissue. As the camel breathes in, the tissue is cooled by the evaporation of water into the dry air. During exhalation, the humid air from the lungs passes this large area of cool surface and much of the humidity condenses to allow reabsorption. The intricacy of the turbinates results in very small distances between the surfaces and the centre of the air stream, which increases the potential for heat and moisture transfer. Inevitably during the heat of the day, a certain amount of water is lost and the cooling created by this process is transferred by blood capillaries to the brain – in extreme conditions keeping this vital organ 6°C cooler than the rest of the camel's body. The camel's kidneys and digestive system are also optimised for water recovery, so that their urine is passed as a thick syrup and their solids are dry enough to light Bedouin fires. A number of engineers have studied mammalian turbinates in camels and other mammals in order to design better water-recovery heat exchangers.

Desert rhubarb grows in parts of Jordan and Israel where precipitation is as low as 75 mm per year. Its large, round leaves have a distinctive texture that resembles a miniature mountain range over the whole leaf surface. Some botanists have theorised that this morphology, combined with a waxy cuticle, helps to channel water towards the centre of the plant, creating a water regime equivalent to many times the annual precipitation.

Another supreme example of adaptation to scarcity is the thorny devil lizard, which is able to harvest water in two ways: using its feet and the spikes on its back. Its skin is covered with fine capillary grooves so that, if it stands on a damp patch of ground, the water tracks up its feet and towards its mouth by capillary action. When conditions are favourable, droplets of water form on the spikes (in a similar way to the bumps on the fog-basking beetle) and then track along the same network of grooves.

80.   The Seawater Greenhouse in Oman as it looked on completion day

81.   The Seawater Greenhouse one year later

Las Palmas Water Theatre

The Las Palmas Water Theatre (fig. 82) proposed for Gran Canaria in the Canary Islands is a good example of how the challenges of water shortages can be transformed into creative solutions. The island has suffered from declining annual precipitation and, with escalating numbers of tourists, has become increasingly dependent on desalinated water brought in from mainland Spain. As a way of supplying fresh water, this is highly carbon intensive – a combination of fossil-fuelled desalination and an inefficient form of transportation (compared to water delivered in pipes).

The project for the Water Theatre came about through a competition that Grimshaw was invited to enter. The town of Las Palmas is situated on a peninsula with a narrow isthmus, on one side of which are the main hotels and the beach while on the other side is a six-lane road and an unsightly container port. The brief for the competition was fairly open and called for proposals to regenerate the port. The Grimshaw team proposed a lightweight deck over the road to create a new park, and a block of mixed-use accommodation on one of the jetties to shield from view the worst of the port areas behind. While there was no specific requirement to propose solutions to the island's water challenges, the team decided to explore the possibility of a charismatic building that doubled as a form of desalination and a public amenity. Charlie Paton, the inventor of the Seawater Greenhouse, collaborated with them and helped to generate the ideas related to desalination.

As we have already seen countless times in this book, biological organisms evolve to make use of whatever opportunities exist. The Canary Islands offered numerous clues in this regard. Apart from the Garoe laurel tree described already, the islands enjoy a steady wind direction for most of the year. Furthermore, because of their volcanic origin, the islands have very steep sides below sea level, which means that it is economically feasible to install a sea pipe that can reach down to deep water. In this part of the world, the sea temperature 1000 m below the surface is at a steady 8 °C. Solar energy is also plentiful and it became apparent that a scheme could be designed based on a boosted form of the Seawater Greenhouse. Taking as a starting point a system of evaporators and condensers, the proposal was to use solar-heated seawater in the former and the cool seawater in the latter. The enhanced evaporation would create abundant humidity while the condenser surfaces at 8 °C would greatly increase the amount of fresh water that could be captured.

Project Director Neven Sidor proposed that this simple idea be transformed into a celebratory form – a bold arching structure, curved on plan, that would create the backdrop to an outdoor amphitheatre. What would conventionally be a mundane piece of infrastructure, such as a desalination plant, was elevated to the level of architecture. Depending on your perspective, it could be argued that the result was a dramatic public building with a desalination plant that came free or vice versa. Initial calculations suggested that the scheme would produce fresh water using one tenth of the energy of the existing method of supply.

The team strove to achieve the maximum benefits from the cold seawater, so that after passing through the Water Theatre it would still be at a temperature suitable for cooling the mixed-use buildings nearby. By passing the seawater through a heat exchanger it would be possible to create cool, fresh water to use in fountains in the planted courtyards. The sprayed water could itself form a condensation surface for humidity in the air, so that the volume of water would increase and form a surplus for irrigation purposes. These landscaped gardens, richly evocative of the Alhambra in Granada, together with the Water Theatre would create a strong narrative about a precious resource, which we all too often take for granted.

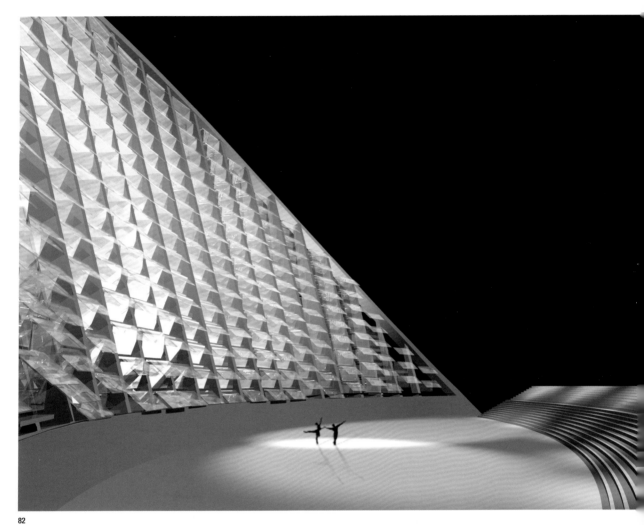

82

82. Las Palmas Water Theatre by Grimshaw – using biomimicry
to transform infrastructure into architecture

Over-abundance

Amory Lovins once joked that 'to an average civil engineer, water is just cubic metres of nuisance to be taken somewhere else in big concrete pipes'. In most cases there are more imaginative approaches to managing surplus water that offer multiple benefits – lower construction costs, minimising flood risk, creating water habitats rich in biodiversity, recharging groundwater and so on. The Biomimicry Guild, working with architects HOK, adopted a more holistic and imaginative approach to resolve the challenges of building in the Lavasa region of India, which experiences 11 m of rain a year – most of which falls in just three months.

The essence of the solution that they devised was to design the buildings with roof structures that would maximise evaporation rather than the more conventional approach of channelling rainwater efficiently into gutters and downpipes (fig. 83). This idea emerged after a detailed study of the local ecology and the way that water flows through it.[61] They concluded that in the native forest as much as 30 per cent of the rain that falls stays up at the canopy level and is evaporated back into the atmosphere. In rainforest environments, it is often the case that water evaporated from the surface of the sea and carried inland as vapour by the wind falls multiple times. In this respect forests near the coast act as atmospheric pumps that help to push precipitation deep into the continental interior, and this reinforces the importance of maintaining these natural cycles. The requirement for maximising evaporation became a significant driver of the architectural form, leading to cascading roof surfaces made from absorbent material. The storm-water-management design continued into the design of all the urban surfaces in order to limit run-off and enhance infiltration and the recharging of groundwater.

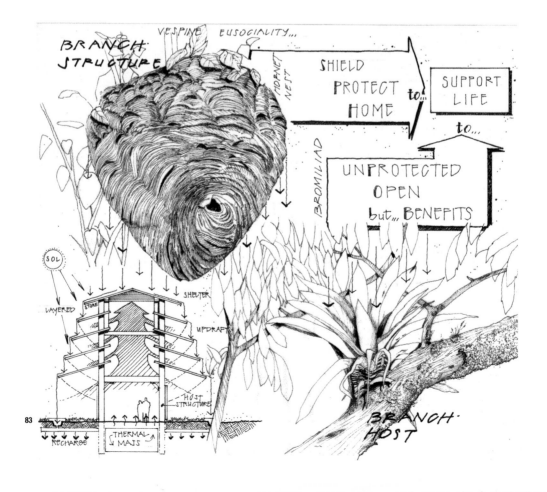

Waste-water treatment

If we were to take a cool, strategic look at the global cycling of all nutrients, it is quite likely that it would lead to some significant changes in the way in which we treat waste water. Over the last half century alone, we lost vast quantities of minerals from the world's soils in the linear flow of nutrients via food, the human gut and our dominant waste-water treatment paradigm. Between 1940 and 1991, this translated directly into a drop in the mineral content of food, with one comprehensive study showing a slump of 19 per cent in magnesium, 29 per cent in calcium, 37 per cent in iron and 62 per cent in copper.[62] Given that current fertiliser production relies very heavily on fossil fuels as a feedstock, and that the supplies of compounds such as phosphates are dwindling, there is a strong case for transforming our food production and water-treatment systems from linear, wasteful, polluting flows to closed-loop solutions. This may well lead to buildings with distinct systems for solid and liquid wastes, using source-separating toilets.[63]

One such technology is called a Living Machine®, (fig. 84) which uses a complex ecosystem of plants and microorganisms cultivated in wetland beds to treat sewage or industrial waste water to a level that allows

84.

83.   Sketch of the Lavasa project by Architects HOK showing how locally adapted species, such as the bromeliad, provided a number of sources of design inspiration including the idea of cascading roof surfaces to catch and evaporate rainfall

84.   A Living Machine®, at the Adam Joseph Lewis Center for Environmental Studies Oberlin College by William McDonough + Partners, that uses plants and micro-organisms to treat waste water

it to be reused locally for toilet flushing, irrigation or reintroducing into the environment. The idea of using versions of wetland ecosystems to treat waste water was first conceived by biologist Dr Käthe Seidel at the Max Plank Institute in the early 1950s. The concept was subsequently pursued further by a number of ecological designers, including Dr John Todd, and then commercialised by Worrell Industries.[64] The systems are the antithesis of a centralised approach, and come much closer to the kind of decentralised, local and resilient ways in which water is cycled in nature. Whereas the former involves heavy infrastructure and complicated 'end-of-pipe' solutions, Living Machines® avoid long distance transportation and often unnecessarily high standards of treatment (when the end use may not be human consumption). The systems are so effective at controlling pathogens, odour and other nuisances often associated with waste water that several Living Machines® have been installed in reception areas of commercial buildings.

Other biomimetic solutions to water treatment include Vortex Process Technology, aquaporin water purification and the Biolytix water filter. All three use ideas derived from biology (vortices and gaseous exchange in the first case, mammalian kidneys for aquaporin and soil microbes in the third example) and could provide viable solutions in building projects although, as self-contained technologies, they are unlikely to contribute to architectural forms and spaces in the way that Living Machines® can.

Water transport

In large animals it is estimated that transporting fluids around the organism's body can use around a sixth of the resting metabolic energy, so it is no surprise that the process of evolution has refined these systems to use as little energy as possible.[65]

85

The biologist C.D. Murray developed a formula (now known as Murray's Law) that describes the relative diameters of branching vessels, and which appears to hold true for most circulatory and respiratory systems in animals as well as the branching of xylem in plants. Murray's Law states that the cube of the radius of a parent vessel that branches symmetrically into two daughter vessels will equal the sum of the cube of the radii of the daughter vessels. More recent studies, building on Murray's work, have shown remarkably consistent angles between bifurcating vessels of around 77 degrees, suggesting that this also represents a minimum-energy solution.[66] There could be substantial savings achieved in designing human-made pipework and ductwork installations to follow the formulae found in biology rather than those taught in schools of mechanical engineering. To date, this does not appear to have been explored or quantified.

Conclusions on managing water

Just as with our use of fossil fuels, many of our standard approaches to water have an inherent technological laziness to them that has developed from the same assumptions of limitlessness that characterised our attitude to other resources at the start of the Industrial Revolution. Studying adaptations in biology can reveal solutions to some of the most intractable of problems, like harvesting water in the desert, a greenhouse that reduces water usage by a factor of eight and schemes such as the Las Palmas Water Theatre that deliver fresh water with a factor-10 saving in energy. Rethinking our waste-water-treatment methods could help restore the fertility of our soils, and re-plumbing buildings and cities with energy-optimised systems could deliver further increases in resource efficiency.

85. The biologist C.D. Murray found that the relative diameters of branching vessels in animals and plants, and the angles formed by the junctions, follow consistent mathematical formulae that suggest a minimum energy system. Architects and engineers could apply the same principles to duct and pipework systems

Chapter FIVE

How will we control our thermal environment?

HOMOEOSTASIS, the tendency for living organisms to maintain steady conditions, is one of the features that most closely link the buildings we create with biology. The similarities break down over the fact that animals tend to continually modify their structures or their behaviour in order to make use of free energy (such as the wind or the steady temperature of the ground), whereas we use large amounts of energy to pump heating or cooling around. In terms of physical control, biological solutions are often complex, multi-functional and highly responsive while ours tend to be simple and relatively unresponsive, and the array of necessary functions are generally handled separately by mono-functional elements.

In this chapter we will be focusing primarily on one aspect of homoeostasis, and that is thermo-regulation. For convenience, we will divide this topic into 'keeping warm' and 'keeping cool'. Of course many organisms have evolved ways to do both, sometimes using the same biological structures. For instance, fossil records of the plate-like structures on the backs of dinosaurs such as the stegosaurus show that they were richly vascular and may have been used for both absorbing and shedding heat, depending on whether the creature positioned itself side on to the sun or to face the wind. In other cases, the characteristics of the habitat to which an organism has adapted have resulted in one strategy being more pronounced than the other.

86.   The communal nests of the Eastern tent caterpillar – an example of insulation and solar orientation producing temperatures inside the nest 4°C above ambient

Some animals, known as homeotherms, generate heat from within and keep their bodies at a steady temperature, while poikilotherms absorb heat from their environment and allow their body temperature to vary quite widely. A brief dip into the history of environmental engineering shows that humans have been growing increasingly demanding in what we regard as a comfortable temperature band in our buildings. This can reach levels of absurdity when, in certain parts of the world, office buildings are heated to 24 °C in winter and cooled to 19 °C in summer. The energy implications of this are huge, so reversing this shift and encouraging clients to tolerate a wider thermal comfort envelope is a critical first stage in designing a low-energy building. This can normally be done with thermal-modelling exercises rather than trying to persuade clients to evolve into poikilotherms or thermophiles.[67]

Keeping warm

The two main sources of heat for organisms are both based on solar energy: firstly direct solar gain and secondly indirect, through metabolising food. Perhaps some of the most elegant examples of trapping solar energy in biology are found in the communal nests built from multiple layers of silk by Eastern tent caterpillars (*Malacosoma americanum*) that face southeast to capture the morning sun. The combination of insulation and solar orientation maintains the temperature inside at least 4 °C above ambient.[68] Termite mounds, often built in areas with widely varying temperatures,

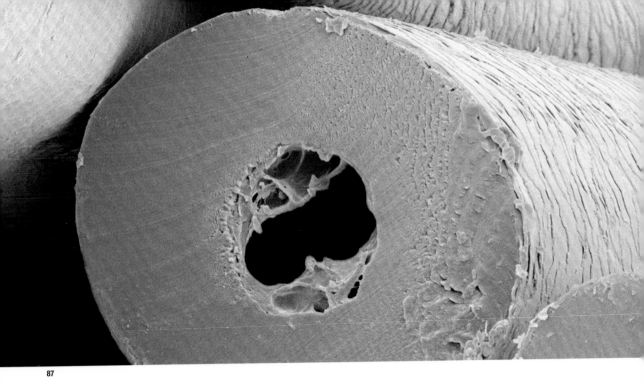

effectively stay warm or cool as required, but have mainly inspired solutions for cooling buildings – so we will turn to these later in the chapter.

The continual generation of heat from metabolism results in many biological solutions for keeping warm being based on reducing heat loss and, for land mammals in temperate regions there are two main physiological ways in which this is achieved: a subcutaneous layer of insulating fat and a dense layer of fur. Those like the polar bear and the reindeer that live in colder regions have further adaptations, such as hollow hair fibres for added insulation (fig. 87). Reindeer fur includes a very dense under-layer of fur that traps air against the skin to reduce convection loss, while longer, 'guard' hairs minimise wind chill by repelling water. For many years, polar bear hair was thought to conduct sunlight down to the black dermis as a kind of solar-heat-gathering adaptation, but this later proved to be a myth. This misconception even inspired some architects and engineers to design wall systems that mimicked the polar bear, using a black-painted wall behind an insulating glass product that employed hollow filaments between two layers of glazing. The system needed a layer of controllable louvres on the outside to prevent overheating and consequently proved to be rather expensive. If it worked (economic issues aside) it would be a perfectly valid way of creating a low-energy solution but, for the pedantically minded, this would be more accurately described as bio-mythologically-inspired rather than biomimetic design. There are also some examples of insulation found in the plant kingdom, such as the groundsel trees that grow on the slopes of Mount Kenya. They accumulate a thick layer of dead leaves from previous years that provide insulation to the trunk and prevent water within the vascular tissues from freezing.

Penguins have evolved plumage (fig. 88) that allows them to respond to two very different conditions. While swimming, the bird's feathers are held flat against the body for optimum streamlining; on land, the penguin lifts its feathers so that the mass of downy filaments at the base of each forms millions of pockets of trapped air for effective insulation.

Insulation is, of course, nothing new in buildings. Perhaps the most important lesson we can learn from penguins is about adapting to different conditions.

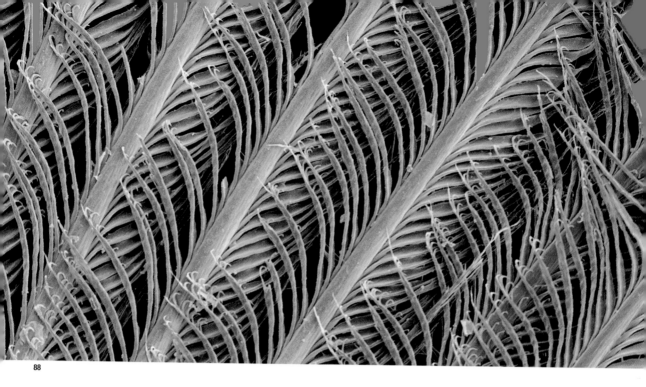

88

Our building skins tend to stay the same regardless of whether there is blazing sun or a night-time blizzard. Penguins huddle together in large groups to minimise their effective surface area, and we could apply similar principles to groups of buildings by connecting them with atria that can be opened in summer to increase ventilation or closed in winter to reduce heat loss. This translation of ideas is more one of analogy than technology, but is valid nevertheless. One very promising technology that is closer to the idea of adaptive skins is the 'SolaRoof' developed by inventor Rick Nelson and engineer Bill Watts. SolaRoof involves creating an approximately 750 mm-deep cavity between two clear layers of polymer and, when additional insulation is required, filling the cavity with bubbles made from a simple soap solution. The bubbles are roughly 6 mm in diameter and are directly equivalent to the air pockets created by penguin feathers, producing millions of static bodies of air between the interior and the exterior. The creators of SolaRoof claim a factor-10 saving in energy compared to conventional twin-skinned polymer roofing.

What we need to see is adaptive technologies spreading from niche applications to mass-market ones. If we could dramatically reduce heat loss from buildings then we could increasingly implement what has been achieved in some PassivHaus projects, in which the heating system has been completely 'designed out' by getting the internal heat gains from the occupants' metabolism and from the equipment in the building (analogous to metabolism) to balance the heat losses through the skin. Reaching these points of whole-systems optimisation is often where quantum changes in energy performance can be achieved.

87. Hollow hair fibres in polar bears – an adaptation that enhances insulative performance

88. Penguins can lift their feathers so that the mass of downy filaments at the base of the shafts create millions of pockets of static air which provide very effective insulation

89

90

Keeping cool

Heat is transferred in four ways: radiation, evaporation, conduction and convection. Many organisms that live in hot regions go to great lengths to avoid picking up heat. Some of them avoid radiative gain by staying out of the sun altogether or skipping across the sand rapidly to minimise absorbing heat through conduction. Applying the same logic to architecture would lead to the conclusion that avoiding heat gain should be the first priority when trying to keep a building cool. In spite of the obviousness of this statement, solar shading has not been exploited anywhere near as widely in late twentieth-century architecture as it could be. Schemes such as the Cabo Llanos Tower in Santa Cruz de Tenerife, Spain, (fig. 89) by Foreign Office Architects and the Singapore Arts Centre (fig. 90) by Michael Wilford with Atelier One and Atelier Ten, both loosely based on plants, give a sense of what can be achieved.[69] The work of Chuck Hoberman in the field of deployable shading structures also shows the beauty of adaptive approaches to solar shading. As I argued in the section above, we have to

develop buildings that adapt to changing conditions if we are to truly mimic the low-energy ways in which biology works.

The World Water Headquarters (fig. 91) designed as a competition entry by Exploration with Charlie Paton proposed two methods of keeping cool: firstly through the evaporation of seawater at the front of the building (as in the Seawater Greenhouse) and secondly through a more extreme version of the fog-basking beetle's radiative cooling. Radiation is the process by which heat diffuses from a warm body to a relatively colder one, and on a clear night it is possible to get a matt black surface to radiate to outer space. The temperature of outer space is absolute zero (minus 273 °C), which means it is hard to beat as a heat sink and explains why clear winter nights are much colder than cloudy ones – on a clear night there is nothing to stop the ground radiating to outer space. The ancient Persians used this principle to make ice in the desert by forming shallow ceramic trays, with a matt black glaze, that

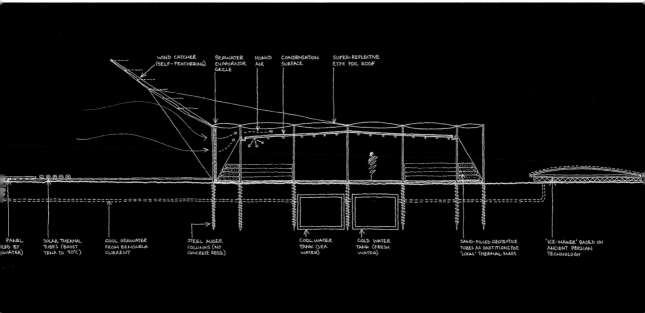

WIND CATCHER
(SELF-FEATHERING)

SEAWATER
EVAPORATOR
GRILLE

HUMID
AIR

CONDENSATION
SURFACE

SUPER-REFLECTIVE
ETFE FOIL ROOF

PANEL
LED BY
WATER)

SOLAR THERMAL
TUBES (BOOST
TEMP. TO 90°C)

COOL SEAWATER
FROM BENGUELA
CURRENT

STEEL AUGER
COLUMNS (NO
CONCRETE REQD.)

COOL WATER
TANK (SEA
WATER)

COLD WATER
TANK (FRESH
WATER)

SAND-FILLED GEOTEXTILE
TUBES AS PARTITIONS FOR
'LOCAL' THERMAL MASS

'ICE-MAKER' BASED ON
ANCIENT PERSIAN
TECHNOLOGY

91

could hold a layer of water. These were put out on clear nights on top of a bed of straw, to minimise heat conduction from the ground, and the radiative temperature loss was enough to make the water freeze. The ice was gathered before sunrise and used to make sherbet. The World Water Headquarters uses the same idea on a bigger scale, together with an underground tank to store the cold water for use during the heat of the day.

Evaporation is an extremely effective means of cooling because water's specific heat capacity is relatively high and therefore large amounts of heat can be dissipated with small amounts of water. The microscopic pores (stomata) on plant leaves control the rate of evaporation and the exchange of gases involved in photosynthesis. When temperatures increase the stomata open wider, which causes more water to evaporate and allows the plant to stay cooler than its surroundings. In extreme cases the leaves wilt, which has the effect of reducing the amount of leaf surface presented to the sun. The water in plants

is transported through vascular bundles in a process known as transpiration, and this is driven by osmotic pressure and capillary action. Capillary action refers to the way that water will spontaneously rise through narrow tubes, such as the xylem vessels in plants, or porous materials; it occurs owing to intermolecular forces between the water and the surfaces with which it is in contact.

89. Cabo Llanos materplan in Santa Cruz de Tenerife, in Spain, by Foreign Office Architects – with palm-leaf inspired shading fins that follow the movement of the sun

90. The Singapore Arts Centre designed by Atelier One, Atelier Ten and Michael Wilford & Partners, showing what can be achieved with shading systems based on plants

91. The World Water Headquarters by Exploration – using the evaporation of seawater and the ancient Persian art of ice-making to keep the building cool

How will we control our thermal environment? **81**

92

93

92. Entry for the IHub competition designed by Jerry Tate
    Architects. The scheme explored the idea of a self-cooling
    building based on transpiration

93. Elephants use their richly vascular ears to shed heat –
    sometimes spraying them with water from their trunk to
    enhance evaporative cooling

94. Roof system designed by Salmaan Craig using BioTRIZ.
    Most sunlight is reflected during the day and at night the
    structure is able to lose heat by radiation at night

Jerry Tate Architects explored the potential of
using transpiration in its IHub competition scheme
(fig. 92). The aim was to create a building that cools
itself using water but without pumps. If capillary
action and an equivalent of transpiration pull could
be harnessed to deliver the water, then the rate of
evaporation would drive the process. There would also
be a close match between the demand for cooling and
the rate at which it was supplied, because hotter days
would create higher rates of evaporation. The designs
show a network of capillary tubes on the southern
elevation through which air can be drawn and cooled
by evaporation. The team's research into the feasibil-
ity of the proposal is at an early stage and the task of
creating long capillary networks appears challenging,
but it's a line of enquiry well worth pursuing. It may be
that an interpretation of electro-osmosis (a naturally
occurring form of osmosis induced by an electric field)
could provide solutions, together with bio-utilisation of
plants as evaporating surfaces.

Apart from the dinosaur back-plates mentioned
above, there are various other interesting examples
of biological structures used for thermo-regulation

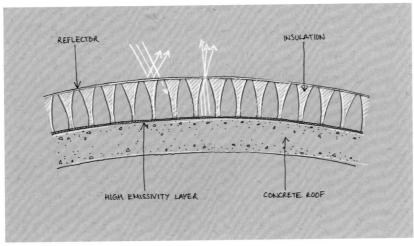

REFLECTOR   INSULATION

HIGH EMISSIVITY LAYER   CONCRETE ROOF

94

through radiation and convection. The generously beaked toco toucan, for instance, has the ability to moderate blood flow to its bill and, by doing so, control the amount of heat dissipated through it. Elephants employ radiation, convection and evaporation when they use their huge ears to lose heat (fig. 93). The ears are permeated by blood capillaries, and elephants enhance heat loss by spraying their ears with water and flapping them. Could buildings have the equivalent of large, flapping, evaporatively cooled elephant ears? Why not – just be careful how you pitch it to the client.

One particularly inventive approach to keeping buildings cool has been devised by engineer Salmaan Craig using a powerful problem-solving methodology known as BioTRIZ. The forerunner of this technique was TRIZ (a Russian acronym for 'Theory of Inventive Problem Solving') developed by an Uzbek engineer and researcher by the name of Genrich Altshuller (1926–98). Any problem can be defined in terms of 'I want A, but it is prevented by B', which is very similar to the German philosopher Hegel's encapsulation of the challenge being one of thesis, antithesis and synthesis. The resolution, in Hegel's terms, was something that managed to combine thesis and antithesis. Altshuller analysed thousands of patents and distilled from these 40 inventive principles, each of which has the potential to be a synthesis (in Hegel's terms). TRIZ has apparently been taught to all Russian schoolchildren since it was

developed by Altshuller, and some have linked this to the Russian's superior inventiveness during the space race with the United States.[70] Julian Vincent and his colleagues, Drs. Olga and Nikolay Bogatyrev at the University of Bath, extended Altshuller's work by studying roughly 2,500 examples of how problems are solved in biology and producing a refined matrix of inventive principles based on their conclusions.[71] Returning to Salmaan Craig, the thesis / antithesis he defined was a roof that was insulated against the sun but that allowed itself to radiate infrared heat at night. Whereas conventional technology would often have pointed towards manipulating energy in some way (such as air conditioning) to solve the problem, BioTRIZ indicated that the synthesis found in biology at this scale would most commonly involve modifications to structure. This led to a way of structuring a layer of insulation on top of a concrete roof that blocked most of the sunlight while funnelling the long-wave radiation with reflectors towards transparent apertures (fig. 94). Test panels demonstrated the potential for the roof temperature to drop as much as 13 °C below ambient by entirely passive means. The concrete would act as a heat store, so that it would radiate this coolness to the rooms below during the day. Craig estimates that the biomimetic roof would maintain the concrete at an average of 4.5 °C cooler than a standard roof in a climate such as that of Riyadh, Saudi Arabia.

Case Study
Compass Termites and the Eastgate Centre

In terms of relative scale, the mounds built by termites (fig. 95) dwarf even the tallest of human skyscrapers. Furthermore, the termites' buildings use zero-waste construction methods, employ solar-powered air conditioning and even boast sustainable agriculture. The forms of the mounds vary according to location. Those of the African species *Macrotermes bellicosus* comprise multiple cathedral-like spires in the hot, dry savannah regions and lower, domed mounds in the cooler forest. According to contemporary biologist Judith Korb and the 1960s entomologist Martin Lüscher, the forms of termite mounds can be explained as elaborate systems for thermal control in order to create optimum egg-laying conditions for the queen termite and ideal temperatures for fungus farming.

From an architectural perspective, perhaps the purest manifestation is the mound created by compass termites (*Amitermes meridionalis*) in Western Australia. The compass termites' tower forms a flattened almond shape in plan, with the long axis aligned perfectly north–south. The long, flat sides present a large absorbing area, which catches the warmth of the morning sun after the cold night, while in the middle of the day the minimum surface area would be presented to the noontime sun. Ventilation tubes within the walls can be controlled by the termites, so it is proposed that if the temperature inside rises too high, vents can be opened and the warm air rises by stack effect. This in turn draws in air through tunnels at ground level, so that the interior mound is moderated by the steady temperature of the ground below the surface. Further tunnels extend all the way down to the water table, so that in extreme conditions termites can carry pieces of leaf down to pick up droplets of water and bring them back to spread on the internal walls to enhance evaporative cooling. Some commentators have claimed that temperature in the royal chamber is maintained within one degree of 31 °C even though the outside temperatures vary by as much as 39 °C between night and day.[72] More recent research (to which we will return) has called this into question somewhat.

Termites were the primary source of inspiration for architect Mick Pearce when he designed the Eastgate Centre in Harare, (fig. 96) Zimbabwe, in conjunction with engineers at Arup (completed in 1996). This office building and shopping complex achieves remarkably steady conditions all year round without conventional air conditioning or heating, and uses only ten per cent of the energy of a standard approach. Pearce studied the mounds of the *M. Michaelseni* and *M. Subhyalinus*, which appear to use a combination of steady ground temperatures and wind-induced natural ventilation as their means of thermo-regulation.

The building is of heavy masonry construction, with external shading devices that minimise solar gain. As in many locations to which termites are adapted, the night-time temperatures drop sharply in Harare and this cool night air is drawn into a plenum between the first and second floors with fans. The cool air is circulated into large floor voids, which contain a labyrinth of precast concrete elements that maximise heat transfer by having a large surface area. During the day, an induced flow system draws air from these cool voids out into the office space via grilles. Warmer air at soffit level, particularly from around the light fittings, is funnelled into 48 masonry chimneys. On all but completely still days, the wind velocity at the top of the chimneys is higher than the velocity at ground level and the effect, enhanced by the positive buoyancy of the warm air, is to draw air upwards. Low-speed fans provide back-up to ensure that there is always adequate ventilation. While outside temperatures typically range between 5 °C and 33 °C, the interior is maintained at 21 °C to 25 °C.

95

96

95. Compass termite mounds – zero waste construction with
    solar powered air-conditioning

96. The Eastgate Centre by architect Mick Pearce – a building
    inspired by termite mounds that maintains comfortable
    conditions close to the equator without mechanical cooling

Recent work related to termite mounds

Recent, very detailed research into termite mounds by Rupert Soar and J. Scott Turner has cast some doubt on the previous accounts of exactly how they work. Soar has shown that the internal temperatures are nowhere near as stable as previously thought, and that the main source of thermal stabilisation is the ground rather than induced-flow ventilation or evaporative cooling. His studies have suggested that termite mounds exploit the wind in much more complex ways than simple stack effect or wind-induced ventilation. Soar and Turner assert that the network of tubes functions more like lungs that facilitate gaseous exchange. It appears that, rather than a simple,

unidirectional flow of air through the mounds, the movement is much more one of ebb and flow and is driven by subtle wind pressure and frequency differences.

Does this mean that any architectural strategies we have developed from an imperfect understanding of termite mounds are therefore bio-mythological rather than biomimetic? I don't think we should worry unduly about this distinction as long as they work and we endeavour to use the latest advances in biological knowledge to make future versions work even better.[73] At the moment, it appears that the studies into termite mounds have some way to go before they arrive at firm conclusions about the best way to translate these lessons into architectural

solutions. We may also find that some solutions that work at the scale of a termite mound may not work at the scale of a building.

One scheme that definitely does work is the Davis Alpine House at Kew Gardens (fig. 97 & 98) by architects Wilkinson Eyre with environmental engineer and termite expert Patrick Bellew of Atelier Ten. It is common for alpine plant collections to be displayed on refrigerated shelves or in fully air-conditioned enclosures, but the client was very keen for the team to generate a more creative solution in this case. The team designed the building to include a thermal labyrinth, which in layman's terms is a basement with a network of masonry walls to create a very large area of thermal mass. This mass can be ventilated at night when temperatures are lower in order to create a store of 'coolth' that can be drawn from during the day by circulating air into the growing area. This approach, sometimes referred to as 'decoupled thermal mass', differs from conventional approaches of exposing heavy wall surfaces within buildings (i.e. 'coupled

97. The Davis Alpine House at Kew Gardens by Wilkinson Eyre and Atelier Ten. Ideas from termite mounds were employed to create the cool conditions necessary for the collection of alpine plants

98. Section through the Davis Alpine House showing the termite-inspired thermal labyrinth in the base of the building

thermal mass') in that the mass can be cooled to below the temperature required for the space that is being served. This allows effective control so that, similarly to the way in which termites appear to open and close vents to control temperature, the source of free cooling can be drawn from as required. The Davis Alpine House includes a deployable sunshade so that solar gain can be controlled. The system has successfully maintained the conditions required for the plants with only minimal inputs of energy to drive the fans. The short payback period of nine years calculated for the cost of the thermal labyrinth relative to conventional cooling has reduced further, since energy costs have risen faster than predicted.

Stabilising temperatures

As we have seen with termite mounds, using forms of thermal storage is a particularly effective strategy in locations that experience large diurnal swings in temperature. In this respect, termites could have been discussed under both 'keeping warm' and 'keeping cool' and I have described them at some length because of their biomimetic celebrity status. Are there other examples that have been left out of the limelight? The stone plants (*Lithops*) (fig. 99) that live in deserts are low profile not just in the physical sense (protruding only a few millimetres above the ground) but also in the extent to which they have been recognised by

99

the design community. Most of the plant is below ground, benefiting from the stable temperatures below the surface while its translucent surface allows light in to the photosynthetic tissue in the 'basement', so to speak. The temperature in some deserts can drop below freezing at night and soar to 50 °C in the day, so forms of temperature stabilisation can be very effective. A building in a desert location that mimicked the stone plants, with the addition of smart adaptive solar shading, could well create comfortable internal temperatures with no further energy input.

Conclusions on controlling thermal environment

It is in the area of thermal control that I would argue we have lost most in terms of historical intelligence, and still have the greatest strides to make in learning from biology. It is precisely the kind of ingenuity, such as that displayed by the ancient Persian art of ice making, that humans developed prior to the Fossil Fuel Age that we need to reawaken. So far, fairly limited solutions have been derived from nature, but the ones that have been are promising: the insulating-bubble roof system that achieves a factor-10 saving in energy, the self-cooling roof developed using BioTRIZ and the termite-inspired Eastgate Centre that stays cool near the equator without any air conditioning – all show the radical potential that is emerging.

We are likely to see building skins evolving into complex systems that increasingly resemble living organisms. As Rupert Soar has argued, the direction in which we need to be heading is 'toward buildings that are extended organisms, where function and structure meld, and are controlled by the overriding demands of homeostasis'.[74]

99. The stone plant has adapted to survive the extreme diurnal swings in temperature by exploiting the stable temperature of the ground

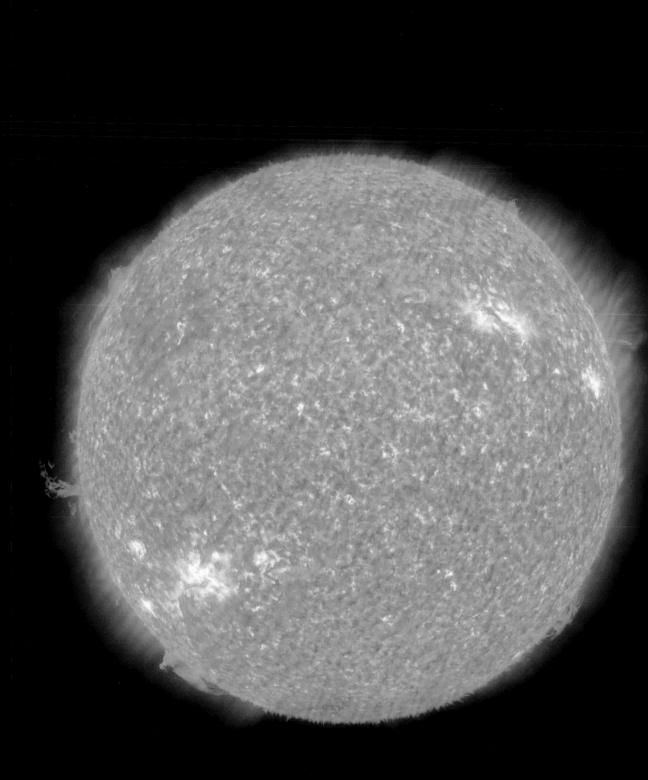

Chapter SIX

How will we produce energy for our buildings?

HUMANS TEND TO tackle problems head-on whereas living organisms, through the process of evolution, have tended to change a problem before resolving it. Nowhere is this more apparent than in the realm of energy. We have generally tried to meet our perceived needs by simply creating more and more energy rather than thinking about how we could develop solutions that, just as in nature, need far less energy in the first place.

Energy is one of our greatest challenges, partly owing to the increasingly urgent realities of climate change and partly to a failure of strategic planning. It is important to have a plan for how we will decarbonise our economies over the course of the next few decades and to understand what that implies for designing buildings and cities. This chapter is less directly involved with buildings than previous ones, but will argue that applying biomimetic principles to energy planning inevitably leads to the notion of a 'solar economy', and that this has significant implications for architects and urban designers. By a 'solar economy' I mean one in which all our energy needs are met with renewable forms of generation. I believe this shift is of critical importance. If we only talk about energy used in buildings rather than where that energy comes from, we would be missing a significant part of what biomimicry can offer and what will be a crucial part of the bigger transformation to an Ecological Age.

Many of the themes that emerged in the earlier chapter about waste and ecosystems thinking are relevant to the discussion here. The same contrast between human-made systems and biology would suggest that a biomimicry solution to energy would involve the following four principles:

- Demand reduction through radical increases in efficiency as the first priority
- A source of energy that will last indefinitely
- Resilience through diversity and distributed networks
- Resource flows that are non-toxic and compatible with a wide range of other systems

Demand reduction, the first step towards a solar economy, is very relevant to the design of buildings because it strengthens the case for all the resource-efficient innovations we have seen in previous chapters. The other three principles are more relevant to larger-scale schemes, such as masterplanning and urban design, because they inform the kinds of technologies that are suitable and the ways in which they should be integrated. We will look at each of the principles in turn below.

100.   The energy received from the sun every year
        represents approximately 10,000 times as much as
        our total annual energy use

Demand reduction

Demand reduction is one area in which innovation through biomimicry offers huge potential. We have seen numerous examples of factor-10 and factor-100 savings in resource use – delivering the same function with a fraction of the resource input. The international consulting firm McKinsey, in their renowned study 'Cost curves for greenhouse gas abatement', concluded that many of the biggest and easiest reductions in greenhouse gas emissions can be found in the built environment. This applies regardless of whether we pursue a nuclear future or a solar-powered future, because most forms of energy-efficiency improvement are cheaper than adding new generating capacity. It is clear from their study that the fastest and cheapest way of cutting greenhouse gas emissions is to aim for a step change in the energy performance of buildings, and then to supply all the remaining energy from low- or zero-carbon sources.

What levels of energy saving are realistically achievable? David MacKay demonstrates how, with current technologies and maintaining a comparable, or arguably better, quality of life, we could reduce our energy demands from 125 kilowatt hours per day per person (kWh/d/p) for the average European down to a figure of 68 kWh/d/p.[75] With biomimicry, there is a real chance that we could take this even further. Making materials with a hundredth of the embodied energy of conventional ones and then shaping these into the kind of highly efficient structures we saw in the first chapter could deliver the levels of resource efficiency seen in spiders' webs, songbird skulls and glass sponges. Similarly, if we could steward all of our resources in closed loops, design out the whole concept of waste and create buildings that passively thermo-regulate, then we could achieve really radical reductions in energy use. All of this innovation is within human capabilities. Every unit of energy saved will make the overall task of decarbonising our economy easier.

Energy sources

If we look at the flows of energy in nature, we find that biological organisms run entirely on current solar 'income'.[76] Could we do the same, and transform from a fossil-fuel global economy to a solar economy? There are many people that would scoff at such an idea, but if one looks at the amount of energy available it brings the possibilities into perspective. The energy received from the sun every year represents approximately 10,000 times as much as we currently use.[77] This bountiful source of energy has sustained life on earth for billions of years, and could supply all our needs.[78] It is therefore not correct to claim that a nuclear-powered future is our only option.[79] Building concentrated solar power plants over roughly five per cent of the world's deserts would be enough to provide for all of our energy needs.[80]

The term 'solar economy' was popularised by the German environmentalist MEP Hermann Scheer, who used it to refer to an economy powered by all forms of renewable energy.[81] This includes direct forms of solar energy like photovoltaics and concentrated solar power; indirect forms of solar energy like wind, wave and biomass; and, somewhat tenuously, tidal and geothermal energy.[82]

Biomimicry has been applied to the design of a number of renewable-energy technologies, and has delivered similar improvements to those we have seen for building technologies. For instance, a new form of wind-turbine blade, developed by a marine biologist with the engaging name of Dr Frank Fish, was inspired by the tubercules on the flippers of humpback whales (fig. 102 & 104). These lumps on the front of the creatures' fins induce vortices which create more lift and allow the whale to maintain manoeuvrability at low speeds.[83] Dr Fish's new blade incorporates the same idea to produce a wind turbine that will maintain operation at slow speeds. The reason this is of radical importance is that all wind turbines have a minimum speed of operation, below which they will stop turning and only start again once the wind speed has picked up enough to overcome inertia. The developers Whalepower Limited claim that the blades can improve output by 20 per cent over a year and result

101

in quieter operation (fig. 103). Further solutions from biomimicry could help address the opposite problem – excessive wind speed, during which wind turbines are generally taken out of operation with automatic braking systems to prevent damage. Many leaves, for instance, change orientation or roll up in high winds to minimise wind loading on the trunk of a tree.[84] If wind-turbine blades were designed to flex, either laterally or longitudinally, under wind loading, then they would present less resistance to the wind.[85] Clearly this means that a smaller proportion of the available energy would be captured in very strong winds, but the big advantage is that the turbine could remain operating in these conditions. This exemplifies one of the key differences between living organisms and engineering (the former is environmentally responsive, while the latter tends not to be), and what can be achieved by following examples from nature.

101. Concentrated solar power uses solar tracking mirrors to focus the sun's heat to drive steam turbines that generate electricity

overleaf

102. Humpback whales have lumps (tubercles) on the front of their flippers which improve hydrodynamic performance at slow speeds

103. 'BioWave' marine energy generators partly inspired by swaying motion of seaweed species in ocean waves

104. Wind turbine blades that mimic whale tubercles in order to maintain energy generation in lower wind speeds

102

103

104

Resilience

Resilience is often defined as the capacity of a system to survive disturbance. In nature, systems have evolved resilience through complex, interconnected networks and a high degree of diversity, such that critical ecosystem functions can be delivered by a number of organisms. Translating this into a discussion about human energy needs would suggest that a resilient system would be one that can provide the required quantities of energy from a diversity of interconnected generation forms. The system would also need to store energy in quantities sufficient to provide for the kind of variability that is inherent in the energy source.

The solar economy starts with the benefit of a constant stream of photons from the sun, and consequently the fluctuation in the availability of energy is constrained. Locally, there are obviously big fluctuations in direct solar energy between day and night; variability in forms of generation, like wind power; and seasonal variations between the rigours of summer and winter. These are the same conditions to which biological organisms have had to adapt, and consequently these all store energy to some extent. Often this is in solid form as sugars, as in the case of tubers, or as fatty deposits in the body tissues of animals. The most common engineering solutions to variability in power sources are batteries and pumped storage schemes (which pump water from a low-level lake to a high level one so that it can be released through turbines when required). The other way in which nature manages fluctuations in energy supply is by simply doing more, in the way of growing or metabolising, when there is energy available and less when there isn't. We can apply the same principles by using smart controls that switch equipment off during short-term peaks, or by varying the cost of electricity to incentivise energy-intensive industries to use more during periods of surplus and less during deficit periods. David MacKay has shown that a combination of these measures – managing demand, pumped storage and batteries in stationary electric vehicles (assuming most transport is electrified) – would be sufficient to deal with the fluctuations that would arise from a solar economy.

Most of our current electricity grid uses high-voltage alternating current (HVAC), which is relatively inefficient in that between seven and nine per cent of the energy is lost in transmission. Increasingly, countries are connecting to each other with high-voltage direct-current (HVDC) cables, which lose only three per cent per 1,000 km. This makes it possible to transmit energy from solar power plants in North Africa to the UK with about the same losses as we have in our conventional AC grids. The advantage of an HVDC super-grid is that a number of countries with a mix of renewable energy sources can be inter-connected, and the diversity of generation and storage forms makes it easier to balance the output of each in terms of timing and quantity. Clearly one country does not have an automatic right to energy from another, so creating the solar economy has to be based on negotiation and fair exchange. Some of the countries that have the highest levels of solar energy are not the most stable, and people might fear the geopolitical implications of being dependent on such countries for energy. Paradoxically, this is where something that is commonly seen as a problem – energy storage – could prove to be a big advantage. The value of this energy, and the fact that it is very difficult to store for longer than a few days, means that there would be great financial incentives for countries with huge solar resources to be consistent providers of solar power and very little to be gained from doing the opposite.

Delivering adequate quantities of energy for the earth's estimated nine billion inhabitants projected for 2050 is by no means an easy matter, and we need to accept that E. F. Schumacher's dictum 'small is beautiful' has its limitations; when it comes to energy generation, 'small' is very often a waste of money. We also need to accept that even with substantial increases in efficiency, we will still need colossal quantities of energy for the growing populations in developing nations – and, as David MacKay has shown, this will either have to come from nuclear or concentrated solar power installed on a massive scale in the world's deserts.

The final points about resilience relate to the energy source and the degree of centralisation or distribution. The energy sources for both fossil-fuel and nuclear generation are problematic. The former contributes to dangerous climate change and the latter is heavily, although not exclusively, dependent on high-grade uranium, which is only found in a few countries and would create significant geopolitical risks in the future if nuclear fission became the predominant form of generation. Atomic energy is characterised by very large output power stations, and such centralised systems are inherently less resilient than more distributed networks because one major incident could conceivably knock out a substantial part of a country's generating capacity.

Compatible systems and resource flows

Elements of a biomimetic system should be compatible with a wide range of other systems in terms of their physical presence and resource flows. An element that produces long-term toxins would be a clear case of incompatibility.

The resource flows in most renewable energy systems are very straightforward. In some cases, heat is captured from the sun or a geothermal source to drive a thermal engine; in other cases, kinetic energy from the wind, ocean currents or waves is used to drive a generator. The energy is produced without the release of any toxins, and in many cases renewable energy installations deliver substantial benefits.

A recent scientific study concluded that the bases of offshore wind turbines create new habitats for crusta-ceans and plants, which can significantly boost numbers of fish.[86] This effect was achieved without any deliber-ate intention, and consequently could be enhanced by designing bases to incorporate holes, crevices and other features to promote biological colonisation. The sugges-tion made above when discussing Biorock™ could push this restorative effect even further, by growing the foun-dations and creating artificial reefs. Then wind farms in coastal waters could function as marine nature reserves as well as energy generators.

Tidal energy offers the benefit of very high pre-dictability of output, because we can reasonably rely on the sun and the moon to carry on doing what they

105

105.   The bases of wind turbines can boost biodiversity and this effect could be enhanced by deliberately designing for colonisation

are doing for the foreseeable future. While the main emphasis to date has been on tidal barrages – effectively a dam across a tidal estuary – it is likely that we will see much more use of tidal lagoons, which have minimal impact on shoreline ecology, fish migration and international shipping. Tidal-lagoon technology offers the same major advantages as those described below for the Green Power Island: energy storage, coastal protection and boosting biodiversity.

Photovoltaic (PV) solar farms and Concentrated Solar Power (CSP) installations will generally be located, for obvious reasons, in regions with high levels of solar intensity, and an intriguing benefit arises. By reducing the amount of direct sunlight that falls on the ground beneath, it makes it possible to grow a range of crops that would not normally survive in the open because of thermal stress and water loss. Grazing animals also benefit from the shade as, in most cases, their natural habitats would have included partial tree cover, and they in turn can build the fertility of the soil. Photovoltaics offer the potential for the skins of buildings to become much closer in function to the photosynthetic surfaces of plants – harvesting energy from the sun so that human-made structures could shift from being static consumers of energy to nett producers of useful resources. At a simpler level, PVs and CSP could provide dual benefits by shading buildings as well as generating energy.

Cultivating algae for biofuels is still in the early stages of development, and many experiments to date have proved to be uneconomic. However, the potential exists for biofuel production to offer valuable by-products. As discussed in the chapter about materials, cellulose can be readily extracted from algae for use in the rapid manufacturing of low-energy materials. Algae cultivation could well prove to be the most effective way of reversing the loss of nutrients from the world's soils – helping to extract minerals from sea water to create micronutrients for human consumption and fertilisers for agriculture. Taking both these secondary benefits into account could make biofuel production far more economically attractive. It is possible that algae production could eventually be deployed on the façades of buildings to provide solar shading and carbon dioxide absorption, but currently the economic viability of this is a long way off.

Case study
The Green Power Island

The Green Power Island, (fig. 106 overleaf) designed by Danish architects Gottlieb Paludan, is a speculative but highly realistic proposal that demonstrates a systems-thinking approach in the way that it integrates a number of renewable energy technologies and energy storage systems in a symbiotic cluster.

The starting point for the scheme is that many forms of renewable energy are variable in terms of their output, and that means of energy storage are needed in order to create a resilient system. It is often the case that low-lying countries best suited to wind-energy deployment are least well suited to building pumped storage capacity because they lack the high terrain normally required for such schemes. The Green Power Island concept overcomes this problem by creating a large reservoir which can be used in the same way: it can be emptied using excess renewable energy and can then generate power, when required, by allowing the sea to flood back in through turbines. The reservoir has a capacity of 22,000,000 m^3, which gives a generating potential of 2.3 Gigawatt hours – enough to supply electricity to all the households in Copenhagen for 24 hours.

The project shows how effectively and compatibly a number of renewable energy technologies can be integrated. The flat areas of the island surrounding the reservoir provide ideal conditions for locating wind turbines – straightforward foundations and clear access to wind. The area below the turbines can be used for growing biomass or food crops. Within the reservoir, a floating array of photovoltaics is proposed which offers the benefit of simple solar tracking – the panels can move in one plane only so that their inclination follows the altitude angle of the sun, while the floating base can rotate to follow the sun's path from east to west. The outer edges of the island provide breeding grounds for seabirds, while the sloping boulder walls below sea level effectively create new rocky shoreline. Whereas flat, rocky seabeds often have relatively low levels of biodiversity, rocky shorelines are amongst the richest habitats that can be found, so this scheme could substantially boost biodiversity and help to rebuild fish stocks.

The location was chosen for its adjacency to an existing gas power station because, during the transition from a fossil-fuel economy to a solar economy, schemes such as the Green Power Island will allow conventional power stations to run at a constant load with consequent improvements in efficiency. The scheme is compatible with a range of other forms of infrastructure, and could be built adjacent to an existing marine causeway. It could also include an industrial harbour and other activities that are best located away from residential areas. Alternatively, the scheme could provide for leisure activities with a marina, allotment gardens and cycle routes.

Most of the world's cities are in coastal locations, and some have been extended by land reclamation. The Green Power Island could be built adjacent to such areas and, in the longer term, provide useful protection for low-lying urban areas against sea-level rise. In many low-lying coastal areas, the greatest risk of flooding comes from large waves breaking over the sea defences. Tidal lagoons or versions of the Green Power Island positioned offshore in such locations would prevent large waves hitting the shore and potentially obviate the need for the expensive job of raising sea walls. While the scheme illustrated opposite was designed for Denmark, the architects have proposed similar schemes for sites in the USA, Bahrain, India and China, with forms of renewable energy best suited to each.

Conclusions on producing energy for buildings

Handled correctly, addressing our energy challenges could drive the greatest wave of innovation that civilisation has ever seen. Any rational approach to cutting greenhouse gas emissions will require radical increases in efficiency as a first step, and innovations in the built environment offer some of the biggest opportunities.

We know from a strategic look at the numbers regarding available energy that it is physically possible to create a solar economy. We also know that there would be major benefits: cleaner air; restored ecosystems, with boosted biodiversity; and nations connecting to share resources, such that energy becomes an issue that promotes cooperation rather than breeding conflict. A biomimetic solution would be resilient, non-toxic, restorative and based on an inexhaustible energy source.

Models for a solar economy suggests that we will need roughly 3.6 million wind turbines, 3 billion domestic-sized PV arrays, some large-scale tidal and hydroelectric schemes and about 600,000 km^2 of CSP – all to be built and installed over the next 40 years. These may sound like daunting figures, but they should be compared with some other manufacturing achievements that we have come to accept as perfectly normal. The 3 billion PV arrays could be compared with the 3 billion mobile phones and roughly the same number of personal computers that have come into existence over the last 20 years. Likewise, the quantity of CSP, hydroelectricity and marine renewables could be compared to the 50 million cars that we make every year,[87] and the 24.5 million tonnes of new ships produced annually by shipbuilding industries.[88] Is creating the solar economy really outside the realm of what modern civilisation has achieved already?[89]

Most forms of renewable energy are still in their infancy, and significant improvements will develop as the technology matures. I believe we will increasingly see renewable energy in symbiotic clusters – offshore wind turbines with bases that also harvest wave energy and incorporate tidal-stream turbines; tidal lagoons with wind turbines on their impoundment walls and wave-energy generation on their seaward sides; CSP installations that also cultivate algae for biofuels and produce methane from waste. If these are to be integrated sensitively into landscapes and cities, then there is a strong case for that being done by architects, engineers and ecologists in collaborative teams. The new infrastructure of the solar economy will present a whole range of design opportunities. It may be that some of the same lessons from biomimicry that are helping to develop more efficient wind-turbine technology will contribute to tidal-stream technology, wave-energy generation and the next generation of photovoltaics, allowing closer integration into the built environment.

Detailed studies by David MacKay have proved that creating the solar economy is practically achievable, although we should not fool ourselves that it will be easy. A vital part of the solution will be concentrated solar power installed on a massive scale, and in the next chapter we will look at a project that explores this form of energy generation.

106. Green Power Island

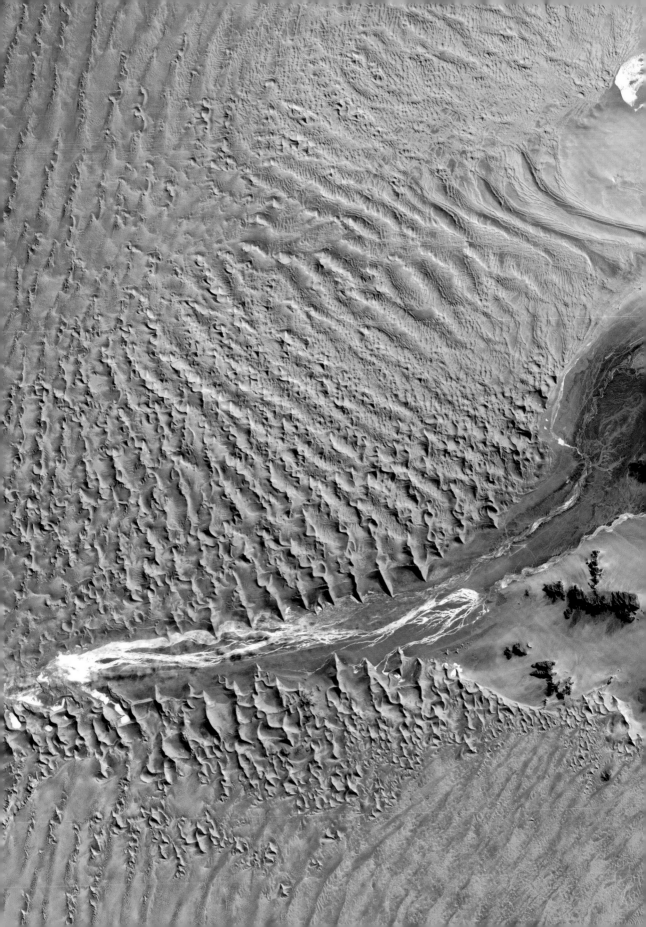

Chapter SEVEN

Synthesis

WHEN PETER SMITHSON was interviewed for the job of running London's Architectural Association in the early 1980s, the idea he pitched to them was as follows: In the first year the students would redesign the world, because when you are 18 you can. In the second year students would design a city. In the third year they would design a major public building. In the fourth year they would design a house, and in the fifth year they would detail it.[90]

The structure of this final chapter is reminiscent of the Smithson anecdote, because we will be looking at how biomimicry has been applied to a large-scale land-reclamation project, an eco-city, a design for a transport terminal, and ultimately to the rethinking of a company and one of the architectural products that it manufactures. While the projects in previous chapters have been characterised by a predominant interest in singular areas of biomimicry, the schemes below are noteworthy for the ways in which they integrate numerous biomimetic strands. The deliberate breadth of project types also conveys a sense of how widely biomimicry can be applied in design and the potential that it offers for addressing future challenges.

107.   It may be hard to believe but large parts of the world's deserts were vegetated a relatively short time ago. The way we steward water, energy and land in integrated ways over the course of the 21st century will have a major bearing on the extent to which our civilization fails or succeeds

A biomimetic land-restoration and energy-generation scheme: The Sahara Forest Project

It may surprise some people that many of the world's deserts supported vegetation in recent history and could do so again if the right conditions could be created. When Julius Caesar arrived in North Africa, what greeted him was a wooded landscape of cedar and cypress trees. The Roman writer Pliny marvelled at the abundance of fruits in the forests and the variety of animals. Caesar's armies set about clearing the land to establish farms, and for the next 200 years North Africa supplied the Roman Empire with half a million tonnes of grain a year, but, over the years, deforestation, salinisation and over-exploitation of the land took its toll. Productivity dropped and the climate changed.[91] It was a highly extractive model of land use, which in many ways became the dominant paradigm for the next two millennia.

Satellite imagery of global photosynthetic activity shows that the boundaries of growth at the edges of deserts shift back and forth quite dramatically over the course of each year. This raises the question of whether interventions can be made at these edges that could halt, or even reverse, desertification. For the team on the Sahara Forest Project, much of the inspiration for tackling this challenge came from studying the organisms that have already adapted to life in deserts. In addition to this, a core biomimicry principle on the scheme was the combining of two proven technologies, concentrated solar power (CSP) and Seawater Greenhouses, for the first time and to explore the potential symbiosis between them.

The synergies between the two technologies are as follows:

- Both technologies work well in hot sunny deserts
- CSP needs a supply of demineralised water to keep the mirrors clean and to run the turbines
- CSP produces a lot of waste heat, which can be used to evaporate more seawater in, or adjacent to, the greenhouses, in order to extend the regenerative benefits
- The CSP mirrors make it possible for a range of plants to grow in the shade underneath and, if the mirrors were placed immediately behind the greenhouse, it could extend the zone of elevated humidity behind and consequently promote more restorative growth
- The greenhouses work very effectively as 'dust scrubbers', removing particles from the air and reducing the build-up of dust on the CSP mirrors

One of the striking things about the first Seawater Greenhouse to be built was that it produced slightly more water than it needed for the plants inside. This surplus, created in a process effectively identical to the Namibian fog-basking beetle that we learned about in Chapter 4, was spread on the land surrounding the greenhouse. The effect of this, combined with the elevated humidity created around the greenhouse, had a striking effect on the site. Prior to the project's construction, the land was largely barren; one year after completion, the greenhouse was surrounded by new vegetation. In this sense, the scheme went beyond 'sustainable' to achieve 'regenerative' design. The aim with the Sahara Forest Project (fig. 108) is to use biomimicry ideas to develop this regenerative aspect to the optimum conclusion.

The initial illustration of the scheme took the form of three strips of greenhouses facing the prevailing wind with tower-type CSP power plants at regular intervals. The three versions of the Seawater Greenhouse that had already been built provided useful performance data, which confirmed that the scheme would evaporate approximately 50 tonnes of seawater per hectare per day. If built on a large scale, equivalent to the 20,000 hectares of greenhouses built in Almeria,

108

southern Spain, the scheme would evaporate a million tonnes of seawater per day. The ideal solution would be for the scheme to operate with minimal energy input, so the possibility of building the scheme in a land area below sea level was explored. A number of these locations exist in North Africa and the Middle East, such as the Qattara Depression and the Dead Sea, which are respectively 100 metres and 400 metres below sea level. Building a version of the Sahara Forest Project in such a location offered the additional benefit of generating hydroelectricity by harnessing the flow in the seawater pipe.

Evaporating vast amounts of sea water would clearly result in large quantities of salts, and, as we saw in Chapter 3, underutilised resources should be seen not as a problem but as an opportunity to add to the

system to create more value. Seawater contains almost every element of the periodic table, and the aspiration is to strive for a zero-waste system by extracting as many resources as possible from the brine. The first thing to crystallise during the evaporation process is calcium carbonate, which builds up on the cardboard evaporator pads in the greenhouses. Once they have become encrusted, the evaporator pads can be taken out and used as lightweight building blocks. The carbon in these blocks would have come out of the atmosphere, into the sea and then been locked away into a building material. The next compound to crystallise is sodium chloride, which can be used for hundreds of industrial applications or simply compressed into another type of building block. Further along the process of extraction comes magnesium

chloride, which is valuable both as a drying agent in air-conditioning systems (one of the lowest-energy ways of cooling air is to evaporate water into it and then use a desiccant to remove the excess humidity) and for the recovery of phosphate from waste water (magnesium chloride combines with the phosphates and nitrates to form a useful fertiliser called struvite). While the commercial extraction of elements like gold is very unlikely to be viable, it should be possible to

108. Sahara Forest Project – a scheme that integrates two
      technologies for the first time to deliver numerous
      synergies and secondary benefits

109

110

extract some of the elements that have been lost from soils through intensive agriculture and return these to desert soils to assist with the regenerative aims of the project. In so doing, the project will be closing an important loop in a system of land use and nutrient management that has been, to a large extent, linear and wasteful since Caesar's time.

The existence of a seawater pipe opens up the possibility of forms of mariculture: abalone farming, algae production, fish cultivation and the growing of halophytes (plants adapted to saline conditions) to name just a few. Apart from providing food (and, in the case of algae, energy), these forms of cultivation could also create secondary products such as cellulose and chitin from which building materials could be made. Growing micro-algae, and macro-algae, could prove to be the most effective way of extracting trace elements from seawater for fertiliser production. Just as we saw with some of the examples of systems thinking, there is a sense in which the system could continue growing, and the more that it expands the greater the number of possibilities.

The team intend to use biomimicry throughout the design and development process. In the future, it may be possible to make mirrored surfaces from proteins at ambient temperature and pressure, as silver Scarabaeidae beetles (fig. 109) do;[92] scratch-free coatings for the mirrors based on the sand skink, (fig. 110) which can 'swim' in sand without suffering from abrasion; linings for the sea pipe that use the same anti-fouling furanones found in seaweeds; and many other innovations that would add to the project.

Often, approaches to environmental challenges involve tackling specific problems when more could be achieved by addressing the systemic failure rather than the individual symptoms. The Sahara Forest Project shows how biomimicry can help to address a whole range of challenges including creating fresh water, shifting to the solar economy, regenerating land, sequestering carbon in soils, closing nutrient cycles and providing employment to large numbers of people.

109. The jewel beetle has a reflective carapace made at ambient temperature and pressure from proteins. Could we learn to make mirrored surfaces in a similar low energy way?

110. The sand skink has evolved to swim into sand and has skin coating with very high levels of abrasion resistance. Could we develop similar scratch proof coatings for mirrors and pieces of equipment?

A biomimetic city: Wanzhuang

Peter Head, who leads Arup's urban masterplanning team, sees biomimicry as crucial to facilitating the transition from the Industrial Age to the Ecological Age. While biomimicry does not address all the necessary sociocultural issues involved in urban design, it is a powerful tool that helps teams to understand the convergent process of delivering ecological design. Head was inspired by the list of principles with which Janine Benyus concludes her book *Biomimicry – Design Inspired by Nature*, in which she states that 'Organisms in a mature ecosystem:

- Use waste as a resource
- Diversify and cooperate to fully use the habitat
- Gather and use energy efficiently
- Optimise rather than maximise
- Use materials sparingly
- Don't foul their nest
- Don't draw down resources
- Remain in balance with the biosphere
- Run on information
- Shop locally[93]

These principles were used extensively in the design of the first eco-city that Arup worked on, Dong Tan, and many of the same ideas were carried through to their work on Wanzhuang (fig. 111) in China.[94] While the site for Dong Tan – a new and growing area of land formed by silt deposition at the mouth of the Yangtze – was highly unusual and allowed a largely technological response, Wanzhuang was a more complicated, and in many ways more typical, context within which to design a new Chinese city. Wanzhuang is an agricultural area, which includes a series of historic villages and pear orchards that are visited by people from all over China. The client's objective was to create an eco-city extension to the nearest urban area, and a previous team had advocated clearing all the existing land uses and imposing a grid of roads and urban blocks.

The members of Head's team started with a careful analysis of not just the physical challenges, such as the poor water quality and low agricultural productivity, but also the culture of the area. They engaged in community consultation and developed a scheme that challenged the conventional *tabula rasa* approach. Arup's aim was to develop a new paradigm, in which urbanism could lift the economy and narrow the economic divide between urban rich and rural poor while allowing the existing farmers to continue farming. The eventual scheme proposed that only 35 per cent of the land would be occupied by buildings and 65 per cent of the agricultural land would therefore be preserved along with 85 per cent of the historic orchards. The new buildings were proposed as five- and six-storey blocks concentrated around the existing settlements, so that nearly all of the village fabric was maintained.

The principle of 'Diversify and cooperate' moved the scheme away from sprawling, mono-functional urban zones towards compact mixed-use layouts that permit people to live, work and learn in close proximity while still allowing immediate access to open spaces for recreation. The resulting concentration of human activities creates vibrant public spaces and makes a range of sustainable transport options viable. New urban developments are often populated with a narrow demographic but the scheme for Wanzhuang would maintain a diversity of ages, cultures and family groups that provide mutual support systems and enhance community cohesion. Local systems for water, energy and waste management allow symbiotic systems to maximise resource efficiency and 'Use waste as a resource'.

The principles of 'Gather and use energy efficiently' and 'Use resources sparingly' led Arup to develop transformative approaches to transport. All freight would be handled through consolidation centres at the periphery that would allow goods to be delivered to the central areas in more efficient ways in order to reduce travel distances and congestion. All vehicles in the urban areas would be either electrically or fuel-cell powered, a far quieter and cleaner alternative which produces consequent health benefits. The improved environmental conditions would also make it possible to naturally ventilate the commercial buildings that would in many cases normally be air conditioned. All the new buildings were proposed to be built to high standards of energy efficiency. The result of these measures was that energy demand was projected to be reduced by 80 per cent, which then made the supply from renewable sources much more achievable.

The discipline of ecological footprinting, which calculates the area of land and sea required to regenerate resources and absorb our wastes, was used by the team to ensure compliance with the principle of 'Remain in balance with the biosphere'.[95] This process revealed the extent to which the productivity of the agricultural land in Wanzhuang would need to be raised. In his Brunel lecture, Peter Head neatly summarised the opportunity that exists here when he said, 'There is a virtuous cycle between using waste as a resource and not polluting the air, water and soil'.[96] At Wanzhuang, the team managed to project a 325 per cent increase in agricultural productivity through improvements in water management, ecologically-based agricultural production and using biodegradable waste as a fertiliser with which to improve soil fertility. Eco-footprinting also revealed the dramatic savings in energy and waste that can be achieved through closed-loop stewardship of resources. At Wanzhuang, the waste materials will be separated at source and delivered to the recycling facility by underground vacuum tubes. Only two per cent will go to landfill and, in time, the hope is that the products that make up this un-recyclable remainder will be redesigned along *Cradle to Cradle* principles.

The author Herbert Girardet has made the point that the typical twentieth-century city was not a 'civilisation' in the true sense of the word but was, and still is, primarily a 'mobilisation of resources, products and people' aimed at maximising consumption.[97] In the design of Wanzhuang, the intention is not maximisation of any one particular criterion but rather an optimised synthesis. Consequently, the approach to transport involves a layout that optimises accessibility rather than designing a transport system that maximises mobility.

It could be argued that some of these solutions are already well-established examples of sustainable design, but what biomimicry provided was a fresh lens with which to look at familiar challenges and a comprehensive framework that promoted the kind of integrative thinking needed in the Ecological Age we are entering. As Peter Head puts it: 'The benefits that accrue are magnified by mobilising the virtuous cycles that connect the environmental, economic and social performance of different components of the built environment so that change in the design of one can lead to benefits in another'.[98]

111

111. Artist's impression of Wanzhuang by Arup

A biomimetic building: 'Island of Light' – Kaohsiung Port and Cruise Service Centre

Similarly to Wanzhuang, the design of Tonkin Liu's 'Island of Light' (fig. 112 & 113) cruise-ship terminal in Taiwan has a cultural starting point. The scheme aims to relate to its context by creating the same sense of connection with nature that is captured by many Chinese landscape paintings. What might have been a perfunctory solution to the requirements for waiting, ticketing and boarding passengers has been elevated to the level of poetic architecture.

There are two main elements to the building: an inclined base containing all the operational accommodation and a lightweight roof canopy, in the form of a forest of tree-like columns, which provides a generous shaded space for the passengers. The architects describe it as follows:

> The structural 'Forest' makes poetry out of the need to create cool space in a hot climate. By day, a filtered, dappled light fills the hall, covering the surface of the 'Hill' and by night the trees glow from within.
>
> The steps which form the inclined surface of the hill are always accessible to the public, both in the glazed climatic zone and on the external steps sheltered by a covered colonnade. The hill invites passengers and the public to be lifted up to a level where they can experience the relationship between the scale of the city and the scale of the ocean liner. From their vantage point the public can watch the theatre of arrival and departure.

Reinforcing the poetic dimensions to the project, the design is based on clear and rational principles of providing comfortable conditions for the building users in a low-energy way. Rather than trying to condition all the spaces, those requiring more stable conditions are contained in the base so that the benefits of thermal mass can be exploited, similarly to the way that animals exploit the steady temperature of the ground. During the hottest times of the year, additional cooling can be circulated through the structure from another locally available source, seawater, using high-efficiency heat exchangers. In the waiting and circulation areas, which can tolerate greater variance in climatic conditions, a soaring canopy of tree structures is created using the shell lace system of perforated steel sheet.

The structural trees perform multiple functions just as real trees do. Firstly, with a covering of ETFE pillows, they provide shelter from the sun, wind and rain. Secondly, they facilitate natural ventilation using rooftop wind-catchers and vents coupled with low-level vents, which combine to exploit the wind and stack-effect forces in order to ensure ample flow of fresh air through the space. Thirdly, the trees control the light – filtering sunlight, bringing light down into the solid base, and, by incorporating luminaires within the structure, creating a glowing symbol for the city at night. Finally, the roof also harvests rainwater to provide the majority of the building's water needs.

The exterior of the inclined base is expressed as a series of horizontal louvres, which create a striated, geological appearance and reflect daylight deep into the spaces behind. In places, these open up to frame dramatic views of the sea.

The scheme therefore employs numerous biomimetic approaches to addressing functional demands, and combines these with richly evocative allusions to the natural environment of Taiwan.

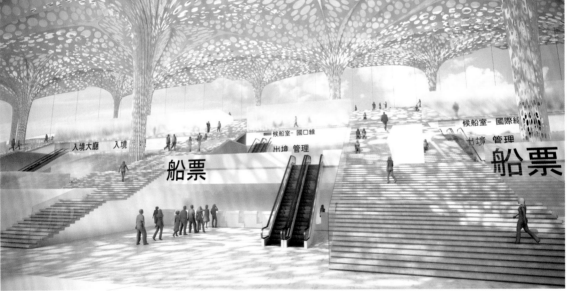

112 + 113

112. External view of Tonkin Liu's 'Island of Light' project showing the 'hill' and 'forest' composition

113. Internal view showing the filigree quality of the 'shell-lace roof' which provides shelter from the sun, wind and rain while filtering the light and harvesting rainwater

A biomimetic company: Interface

In 1994, Interface was a normal, commercially successful company supplying a product, carpet tiles, to architects and clients in the construction and interiors industry. A request came through for the chairman, Ray Anderson, to give a talk about the company's environmental policy, and after some soul-searching about what to say he took the advice of a colleague who recommended reading Paul Hawken's *The Ecology of Commerce*. Anderson describes the experience as being 'like a spear in the chest'.[99] The realisation struck him that there was 'not an industrial company on earth that is sustainable in the sense of meeting its current needs without, in some measure, depriving future generations of the means of meeting their needs'.[100] He decided to set Interface on course to be the first sustainable corporation, and subsequently to become the first restorative company.

What followed was an intensive process of engagement with pioneering thinkers, including Janine Benyus, Paul Hawken, Amory and Hunter Lovins, and Jonathon Porritt, all of whom helped to re-conceive of the company and its mission. Perhaps the most fundamental biomimicry principle that drove innovation was the idea of treating waste as an opportunity. The then President and COO, Charlie Eitel, defined waste in even more incisive terms as 'every measurable input that does not create customer value'.[101]

Traditional approaches to flooring often involved glueing broadloom carpet to office floors, which required all the furniture to be cleared from the spaces. It also led to a cocktail of off-gassing compounds from the adhesives and fire retardants being breathed in by the occupants. After a relatively short period, the carpet would be worn out in some very limited areas of intensive use and consequently would all be pulled up and thrown into landfill, to be replaced by more carpet in an identical process of disruption, expense and internal pollution. Interface recognised that there were huge advantages to be gained from offering a floor-covering service rather than a product. By developing a durable carpet tile that could be reconditioned almost indefinitely, the company could replace worn carpets

out of office hours and provide the client with a better service at lower cost, while achieving radical increases in resource efficiency.

Ray Anderson, in his many speeches, regularly asked the audience to close their eyes and imagine a place of complete tranquility and beauty. He then asks them to raise their hands if their imagined place is outside and then to open their eyes, at which point they discover that nearly everyone in the room also has their hand up. Almost without exception, people picture a forest, prairie, stream or other example of wilderness; evidence of E. O. Wilson's notion of 'Biophilia' and our apparent, deeply held affinity with the natural world. In 2000, Interface worked with the Biomimicry Guild to answer the question of 'How would nature make a carpet?' A workshop was held and the attendees, mainly designers, were sent out into the forest to ponder on this issue. Somewhat baffled at first, the designers thought they should look for shapes of flowers, natural colours and the like. However, one of the key observations that came back to the workshop was 'randomness', particularly the way that no two areas of forest floor are exactly the same and yet it still creates a harmonious appearance. The conclusion of the exercise was a carpet called Entropy™ that mimicked this chaotic pattern, and the huge advantages of this idea unfolded gradually (fig. 114 & 115). Firstly, it could be laid randomly and installation waste virtually disappeared. Secondly, quality-control rejects as good as disappeared as well, because the very idea of 'imperfection' no longer existed. Thirdly, repairs were easier and it became possible to even out occurrences of wear by rotating carpet tiles, because exact matches were impossible anyway. The carpet went on to become Interface's biggest selling range, and it still remains extremely popular.

The waves of biomimetic innovation at Interface have continued, with ways of eliminating adhesives inspired by the gecko's ability to stick to seemingly smooth surfaces. Their designers have used principles of 'fitting form to function' to re-engineer carpets so that they achieved the same durability with half the surface material. Interface has also pushed the

114

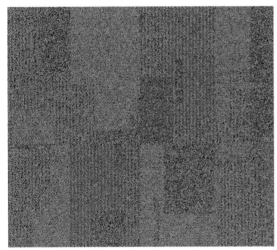

115

114. Interface held a workshop with the Biomimicry Guild who challenged them to think about how nature would design a floor covering. The team were inspired by the random but harmonious appearance of the forest floor

115. The end result of the workshop was Interface's 'Entropy' carpet which, through its random pattern, produced some dramatic benefits

boundaries of social sustainability with ranges like Fairworks™ that combine craft skills and local materials in some of the poorest parts of the world, demonstrating that big business can play a role in poverty alleviation.

Interface has probably applied biomimicry to their whole business culture more comprehensively than any other company and, arguably, has got closer to being a truly sustainable company than any other major industrial player. From 1996 to 2009, the company showed actual reduction of greenhouse gas emissions by 44 per cent from a baseline in 1996, and achieved an 80 per cent reduction in waste sent to landfill.[102] Its vision of the sustainable company that it wants to become by 2020 is one that very closely follows the principles set out in Janine Benyus's book: It would be a company that runs on sunlight, uses only the energy needed, does not overdesign, recycles everything, rewards diversity and cooperation, adapts to local conditions and skills, curbs excess, embraces disruptive innovation and accepts failure as a necessary step in evolving better solutions.

Conclusions

It may seem curious to finish a book about biomimicry in architecture by talking about carpets, but there is a satisfying symmetry to this. It was textile companies that led the world into the Industrial Age, and it is surely all the more appropriate that one of them is now leading industry out, into the Ecological Age.[103] Many architectural product manufacturers are now following similar paths: developing self-cleaning surfaces inspired by lotus leaves, self-repairing concrete, colour effects without pigments and a growing list of other biomimetic innovations. Even in unlikely areas like fire safety, it is possible to find solutions from nature: the bombardier beetle, which repels predators with a high-temperature explosion fired from its abdomen, is being studied to help develop more effective fire extinguishers; the bark beetle, (fig. 116) which can detect a forest fire at 10 km (roughly 1,000 times the range of human-made fire detectors) is pointing the way to better fire sensors; and trees like eucalyptus, which can survive forest fires, could inspire new fire-resistant materials.

We have seen that the notion of a solar economy could be facilitated through biomimetic invention, both directly in terms of shaping more efficient renewable-energy systems and in radically reducing our energy use and, if pursued with CSP in deserts at large scale, could deliver numerous benefits. It is also entirely consistent with the way that nature works in terms of resilience, compatibility and indefinite supply. This is no coincidence. The sun is the source of energy that has supported all life for billions of years.

It would be bordering on the evangelical to suggest that nature has the answer to everything. Nature does not make things out of metals, nor does it have high-speed rotating axles or heat engines. But living organisms, because of the ruthless refinement of evolution, are remarkable models from which we can learn to achieve radical increases in resource efficiency: if we multiply the implications of materials made with a factor-100 energy saving by efficiencies of structures that are ten times higher than conventional approaches, then we glimpse what could be attained. And, if we do it correctly, all of those materials can be cycled permanently in endless transformations. The very notion of waste can be progressively designed out. Much of this may be beyond our current capabilities, but we know that this is not the realm of fantasy because the natural world is living proof of the possibility.

We might reasonably ask, 'How can these transformations be accelerated?' Often, our first response to a question like this is to think of what would compel change and, while there is a place for legal measures in some circumstances, fiscal measures that reward ingenuity are a surer way to stimulate innovation. Such measures are likely to be more consistent with biomimicry – creating the conditions out of which these transformations would emerge. In the process of evolution, some of the most remarkable adaptations have occurred in response to scarcity or to extreme selective pressure that favoured efficiency. We could stimulate innovation in an equivalent way by shifting taxation away from employment and towards the use of resources. It would also incentivise the kind of ecosystems models we saw in Chapter 3 by rewarding 'waste entrepreneurs'. Making resources more expensive, before they become problematically scarce, would be one of the best ways to ensure that those resources are used more efficiently.[104] Often, governments do the exact opposite in order to provide a quick fix. In the future, our indicator of well-being, just as it is in nature, will be abundant and dynamic equilibrium rather than the mirage of maximising GDP.

It could be argued that biomimicry is the logical conclusion of a shift that has gone from attempting to conquer nature, then trying to preserve it and now to striving for a reconciliation in which, using biomimetic principles, we can retain the many wonderful things that civilisation has developed but rethink the things that have proved to be poorly adapted to the long term. Should we be optimists or pessimists when looking to the future? Hans Rosling argues that we should be neither, as both of those positions imply inevitability. What we should be, he says, is 'possibilists'.[105] We should decide on the future we want and then set about creating it. The Ecological Age is now a clear enough destination to aim for, and I hope this book will help all those who want to make that journey.

116

116. Another source of inspiration for biomimetic products in the unlikely area of fire safety. The Melanophila acuminata beetle can detect a forest fire at 10km and is being researched in order to develop detection systems with a longer range that use less energy

overleaf

117. Biomimicry holds a wealth of possibilities for new products. The bombardier beetle which fires a high temperature cocktail of chemicals out of its abdomen as a defence against predators is being studied in order to develop more effective forms of fire extinguisher

The following is intended as an
aide-memoire for students and architects applying biomimicry

General

- Learn to collaborate, which means knowing enough about other disciplines to ask the right questions. There are no short cuts here.
- Bring biologists and ecologists into the design process as early as possible.

Radical increases in resource efficiency

- Define challenges in functional terms and then see how that function is delivered in biology.
- Use BioTRIZ to develop as yet unknown solutions.
- Rethink the problem from first principles, and optimise the whole system.
- Put the material in the right place (use efficient overall structural forms and individual elements that employ shape and hierarchy to maximum effect).
- Design in a way that is both adapted to the specifics of the location and adaptable to changing conditions.
- Look for 'free' sources of energy (the steady temperature of the ground, the cool temperature of deep seawater, reliable wind direction, etc.).
- Design out functions that use energy, through improved information flows.
- If the ideal solution is prevented by the brief, then you will need to apply a lever higher up in the chain of influence (refer to Donella Meadows' essay 'Leverage Points'[106]).

Shifting from linear to closed-loop systems

- Look at underutilised resources as an opportunity rather than a problem – add elements to the system that transform waste into value.
- Widen the system boundaries and connect with resource flows in adjoining schemes.
- Look for synergies between technologies by assessing the inputs and outputs of each.
- Reconsider conventional approaches to resource ownership, and explore opportunities for leasing services rather than purchasing products.

Shifting from a fossil-fuel economy to a solar economy

- Develop a plan for running the scheme on current solar income with numbers that add up. Refer to David MacKay's *Sustainable energy – without the hot air* and work through the implications, which will almost certainly compel you to re-explore every opportunity for radical increases in resource efficiency.
- Think about opportunities for buildings to become nett producers of energy rather than nett consumers.
- To get the economics of solar energy to stack up, offset the cost by fully integrating the systems so that they are part of the skin or structure of the building rather than separate elements.
- Fossil fuels should be used for making high-performance materials, not for burning.

Acknowledgements

THE SEEDS OF MY INTEREST in biomimicry were sown in my teenage years, but emerged fully when I participated in a one-week course at Schumacher College led by Amory Lovins and Janine Benyus in 2003. I am grateful to both the course leaders for the generosity with which they shared their knowledge during what was a truly inspiring week that changed the path of my career permanently. Two other pioneers of biomimicry, Dayna Baumeister and Julian Vincent, became mentors for me while writing this book. Julian provided highly valued input throughout, including numerous readings of drafts, a wealth of important references and corrections to my biological blunders. Dayna emboldened me at key stages with inspirational comments. The photographer Kelly Hill has been a constant source of support, both as my wife and in bringing her skilled eye to the sourcing of images. My editors, Lucy Harbor and James Thompson, have done an excellent job of helping to clarify the text. InterfaceFlor generously funded images from the Science Photo Library which added immeasurably to the visual quality of the book.

I am grateful to all those that have written illuminating books about biomimetics (including all their names here would start to feel like a rerun of the bibliography!) and to others, like Andy Middleton and Graham Dodd, whom I have had the great pleasure of teaching with and learning from. Many individuals have been generous with their time and knowledge in discussing ideas for the book, sharing thoughts or reading drafts, including: Patrick Bellew, Karen Blincoe, David Crooks, David de Rothschild, Herbert Girardet, Brian Goodwin, Frederic Hauge, Peter Head, Geoff Hollington, David Kirkland, Anna Liu, Leonora Oppenheim, Anna Maria Orru, Charlie Paton, Yaniv Peer, Jonathon Porritt, Malcolm Smith, Neil Thomas, Mike Tonkin, Bill Watts and Graham Wiles. I've never met David MacKay, but he did us all a great service in writing his thoroughly researched and wonderfully readable book of numbers. My chapter on energy owes a lot to his work.

I would like to thank Grimshaw for the opportunities I had while working there, and for the input of the Green R&D group which was a wonderful forum for ideas. Somewhat late, I must thank my biology teacher at King James College, Alan Jones, who did so much to convey his enthusiasm for the subject and unwittingly helped me on my career path. Similarly, I am grateful to my parents for their art and engineering nurture and to my uncle, whose gift of the Club of Rome's book *Blueprint for survival* in my early teenage years provided another influential strand to my future development.

I would also like to thank the countless scientists who continue to reveal biological secrets and those who work in environmentally related fields, such as climate science, with the highest integrity and do so in spite of the media assault on their findings. It often seems that 200 years after the age of the Enlightenment we are entering the Endarkenment, in which unqualified sceptics are considered as reliable as scientists on matters of climatology, and monomathic economists create political policies with no regard for natural capital or long-term value. We will need polymaths and inspired collaboration more than ever during the decades ahead.

Bibliography

Derek Abbott, 'Keeping the Energy Debate Clean: How Do We Supply the World's Energy Needs?', *Proceedings of the IEEE*, Vol. 98, No. 1, January 2010, pp.42–66

Hugh Aldersey-Williams, *Zoomorphic: New Animal Architecture*, London, Laurence King Publishing Ltd, 2003. ISBN 1 85669 340 6

Robert Allen (ed.), *Bulletproof Feathers: How Science Uses Nature's Secrets to Design Cutting-Edge Technology*, Chicago and London, University of Chicago Press, 2010. ISBN-13: 978-0-226-01470-8

Ray Anderson, *Confessions of a radical industrialist*, London, Random House Business Books, 2009. ISBN 978-1-847-94028-5

Anon, (no author credit) 'Whales and dolphins influence new wind turbine design', *Science Daily*®, 8 July 2008. http://www.sciencedaily.com/releases/2008/07/080707222315.htm

Anon, (no author credit) 'Offshore Wind Power and Wave Energy Devices Create Artificial Reefs', *Science Daily*®, 19 January 2010 http://www.sciencedaily.com/releases/2010/01/100118132130.htm

Michael F. Ashby, *Materials and the Environment: Eco-Informed Material Choice*, Oxford, Butterworth-Heinemann, 2009. ISBN: 978-1-85617-608-8

Patrick Bellew, 'Going Underground', *Ingenia*, Issue 28, September 2006, pp.41–6

B. Bensaude-Vincent, H. Arribart, Y. Bouligand, and C. Sanchez, 'Chemists and the school of nature', *New Journal of Chemistry*, 2002, 26, pp.1–5. Received (in Montpellier, France) 13 September 2001, accepted 26 November 2001, first published as an Advance Article on the web 3 January 2002

Janine Benyus, *Biomimicry: Innovation Inspired by Nature*, New York, Harper Collins, 1998. ISBN 0-688-16099-9

Janine Benyus and Amory Lovins, 'Natural Capitalism', course at Schumacher College, 23 to 26 September 2003

A. Beukers and E. van Hinte, *Lightness: The inevitable renaissance of minimum energy structures*, Rotterdam, 010 Publishers, 1999. ISBN 90-6450-334-6

J. Chilton, B. S. Choo and O. Popovi, 'Morphology of Some Three-Dimensional Beam Grillage Structures in Architecture and Nature', *Natürliche Konstruktionen 9, Evolution of Natural Structures*, Proceedings of Third International Symposium of Sonderforchungsbereich 230, Stuttgart, pp.19–24

S. Craig, 'Biomimetics design tool used to develop new components for lower energy buildings', unpublished dissertation, School of Engineering and Design, Brunel University, Uxbridge, Middlesex, September 2008

S. Craig, D. Harrison, et al. 'BioTRIZ suggests radiative cooling of buildings can be done passively by changing the structure of roof insulation to let longwave infrared pass'. *Journal of Bionic Engineering*, 5(1): 55–66

J. P. E. C. Darlington, 'The structure of mature mounds of the termite Macrotermes michaelseni in Kenya', *Insect Science and its Applications*, 6, 1986, pp.149–56

D. S. A. De Focatis, and S. D. Guest, 'Deployable membranes designed from folding tree leaves', *Philosophical Transactions of The Royal Society*, London, A 2002 360, pp.227–38 (retrieved from rsta.royalsocietypublishing.org on 21.01.11)

Pooran Desai, *One Planet Communities: A real-life guide to sustainable living*, Chichester, West Sussex, John Wiley & Sons Limited, 2010. ISBN 978-0-470-71546-8

Shiva Dindyal 'The sperm count has been decreasing steadily for many years in Western industrialised countries: Is there an endocrine basis for this decrease?', *The Internet Journal of Urology* 2004, Volume 2 Number 1, ISSN: 1528-8390 (retrieved on 24.01.11). http://www.ispub.com/ostia/index.php?xmlFilePath=journals/iju/vol2n1/sperm.xml

G. K. Dosier, 'Biologically Manufactured Building Materials', abstract submitted for 'Geobiology in Space Exploration' Workshop at Université Cady Ayyad, Ibn Battuta Centre, Morocco, 19 January 2011

Carolyn Dry, 'Development of self-repairing concrete', Natural Process Design Inc. website (accessed 24.01.11) http://www.naturalprocessdesign.com/Tech_Concrete.htm

Karl von Frisch, *Animal Architecture*, London, Hutchinson, 1975. ISBN 0 09 122710 0

J. F. Gabriel. *Beyond the cube: the architecture of space frames and polyhedra*, London, John Wiley & Sons, Inc., 1997. ISBN 0-471-12261-0

Herbert Girardet, *Cities, People, Planet: Liveable Cities for Sustainable World*, Chichester, West Sussex, John Wiley & Sons Ltd., 2004. ISBN 0-470-85284-4

J. E. Gordon, *The New Science of Strong Materials*, London, Penguin Books Ltd, Second Edition, 1976. ISBN 0-14-013597-9

J. R. Gould and C. G. Gould, *Animal Architects: Building and the evolution of intelligence*, New York, Basic Books, 2007. ISBN-13:978-0-465-02782-8

David Grimm, 'Beetles may help battle blazes', *Science*, Vol. 305, 13 August 2004, p.940 (retrieved from www.sciencemag.org on 28.03.11)

S. D. Guest S. and Pellegrino, 'Inextensional Wrapping of Flat Membranes', in R. Motro and T. Wester (eds.), Proceedings of the First International Conference on Structural Morphology, Montpellier, France, 7–11 September, pp.203–15

Ernst Haeckel, *Art Forms from the Oceans*, Munich/Berlin/London/New York, Prestel Verlag, 2005. ISBN 3-7913-3327-5

D. X. Hammer, H. Schmitz, A. Schmitz, H. Grady Rylander A. J. and Welch, 'Sensitivity threshold and response characteristics of infrared detection in the beetle *Melanophila acuminata* (Coleoptera: Buprestidae)', *Comparative Biochemistry and Physiology – Part A: Molecular & Integrative Physiology*, 128, Received 3 August 2000; revised 10 November 2000; accepted 17 November 2000. Available online 26 March 2001, pp.805–19

G. Hammond, C. Jones (Sustainable Energy Research Team, Department of Mechanical Engineering, Bath University), 'Inventory of Carbon and Energy (ICE). Version 1.6a'. http://www.bath.ac.uk/mech-eng/sert/embodied/ (accessed 26.01.11)

Mike Hansell, *Animal Architecture (Oxford Animal Biology Series)*, Oxford, Oxford University Press, 2005. ISBN 0-19-850752-6

Mike Hansell, *Built by Animals: The natural history of animal architecture*, Oxford, Oxford University Press, 2007. ISBN 978-0-19-920556-1

P. Hawken, A. Lovins and L. H. Lovins, *Natural Capitalism*, New York, Back Bay Books/Little, Brown and Company, 1999. ISBN 978-0-316-35300-7

Peter Head, 'Entering the Ecological Age', The Brunel Lecture 2008, The Institution of Civil Engineers 2008 Brunel International Lecture. http://www.arup.com/_assets/_download/72B9BD7D-19BB-316E-40000ADE36037C13.pdf (accessed 03.04.11)

M. Hensel, A. Menges and M. Weinstock, *Emergent technologies and design: Towards a biological paradigm for architecture*, Abingdon, Oxfordshire, and New York, Routledge, 2010. ISBN 10 0-415-49344-7

David Lloyd Jones, *Architecture and the Environment: Bioclimatic Building Design*, London, Laurence King Publishing Ltd, 1998. ISBN 1 85669 103 9

H. Jonkers, 'Bioconcrete', Technical University of Delft website (accessed 24.01.11). http://www.tnw.tudelft.nl/live/pagina.jsp?id=6ce46115-d4b8-4668-a1a4-74c09b6d34ee&lang=en (accessed 18.07.11)

J. Kimpian, 'PneuMatrix – the Architecture of Pneumatic Structures in the Digital World', unpublished PhD thesis dissertation http://kimpian.com/ (accessed 18.07.11)

M. J. King and J. F. V. Vincent, 'The mechanism of drilling by wood wasp ovipositors', *Biomimetics*, 3, 187–201

H. Kobayashi, B. Kresling and J. F. V. Vincent, 'The geometry of unfolding tree leaves' Proceedings of the Royal Society London, B265, 147–54

J. Y. Lee and Æ. S. J. Lee, 'Murray's law and the bifurcation angle in the arterial micro-circulation system and their application to the design of microfluidics', *Microfluidics and Nanofluidics*, Vol. 8, Number 1, 2010, pp.85–95

David J. C. MacKay, *Sustainable Energy – without the hot air*, Cambridge, UIT Cambridge Ltd, 2008. ISBN 978-0-9544529-3-3. Available free online from www.withouthotair.com (accessed 18.07.11)

Claus C. Mattheck, *Design in Nature – Learning from trees*, Berlin/Heidelberg/New York, Springer-Verlag, 1998. ISBN 3-540-62937-8

W. McDonough and M. Braungart, *Cradle to Cradle: Remaking the Way We Make Things*, New York, North Point Press, 2002. ISBN-13: 978-0-86547-587-8

Fiona McWilliam, 'Swat Team: Termite mound construction offers a lesson in natural ventilation for small buildings', *Building Sustainable Design*, September 2009, Vol. 1, no. 8, pp.35–7

Donella Meadows, 'Leverage Points: Places to intervene in a system', Hartland, Vermont, The Sustainability Institute, 1999. Available online at http://www.sustainer.org/pubs/Leverage_Points.pdf (accessed 03.04.11)

Tom Mueller, 'Biomimetics', *National Geographic*, April 2008. http://ngm.nationalgeographic.com/2008/04/biomimetics/tom-mueller-text/1

P. L. Nervi, *P. L. Nervi – New Structures*, London, The Architectural Press, 1963

P. L. Nervi, 'Considerations on the architecture of our time', transcript of the British Italian Society Leconfield Lecture by Pier Luigi Nervi, Pier Luigi Nervi archive folder held at the British Architectural Library, Portland Place, London

David W. Orr, *Design on the Edge: The Making of a High-Performance Building*, Cambridge, Massachusetts, MIT Press, 2006

F. Otto, M. Ansell, B. Baier, M. Barnes, R. Blum, B. Burkhardt, M. Cook, D. Croome, M. Dickson, H. Drüsedau, S. Greiner, E. Happold, J. Harnach, B. Harris, E. Haug, B. Haug, J. Hennicke, J. Howell, I. Lidell, R. Münsch, E. Racah, C. Williams, E. Schauer and D. Schwenkel, *Institute for Lightweight Structures volumes IL1 to IL32*, published by Institut für leichte Flächentragwerke, Universität Stuttgart; School of Architecture and Building Engineering, University of Bath; Universität Essen, Gesamthochschule, Fachbereich Bauwesen, dates from 1971

Gunter Pauli, *The Blue Economy: 10 Years, 100 Innovations, 100 Million Jobs, Report to the Club of Rome*, Taos, New Mexico, Paradigm Publications, 2010. ISBN 978-0-912111-90-2

Yaniv Peer, 'Evolutionary Architecture: Reflections of Nature in a Digital World', unpublished student dissertation, Manchester Metropolitan University, 2007

Anton Peter-Fröhlich, 'SCST – Sanitation Concepts for Separate Treatment', website article, Berlin, Competence Centre, Berlin Water Company. Project funded by the framework of the LIFE programme of the European Union (LIFE03 ENV/D/000025) from 1 January 2003–31 December 2006. http://www.kompetenz-wasser.de/SCST.22.0.html?&L=1&type=title%3Daccelerate (accessed 18.07.11)

Kathryn Phillips, 'Beetles "hear" heat through pressure vessels', *Journal of Experimental Biology*, Vol. 211, no. (16):i–a (2008). First published online, 08 August 2008

Michael Pollan, *The Omnivore's Dilemma*, London, Bloomsbury Publishing PLC, 2006. ISBN 978-0-7475-8683-8

Jeffrey Sachs, *Common Wealth: Economics for a Crowded Planet*, London, Penguin Books Ltd, 2008. ISBN 978-0-713-99919-8

A. E. Seago, P. Brady, J-P. Vigneron and T. D. Schultz, 'Gold bugs and beyond: a review of iridescence and structural colour mechanisms in beetles (Coleoptera)', *Journal of the*

Royal Society Interface, 6, 2009, S165–S184, doi:10.1098/rsif.2008.0354.focus. Published online 28 October 2008

Hermann Scheer, *The Solar Economy: Renewable Energy for a Sustainable Global Future*, London, Earthscan, 2002. ISBN: 1-84407-075-1

Tom Shelley, 'Rapid manufacturing set to go mainstream', *Eureka* magazine, 14 November 2007, http://www.eurekamagazine.co.uk/article/12049/Rapid-manufacturing-set-to-go-mainstream.aspx (accessed 03.04.11)

Lynn Skinner, 'Biomimetics and its Potential Role in Architecture', unpublished student dissertation, The Scott Sutherland School, Faculty of Design and Technology, Robert Gordon University, Aberdeen, January 2005

R. C. Soar and J. S. Turner, 'Beyond biomimicry: What termites can tell us about realizing the living building', First International Conference on Industrialized, Intelligent Construction (I3CON), Loughborough University, 14–16 May 2008

Carolyn Steel, *Hungry City: How Food Shapes Our Lives*, London, Chatto & Windus, 2008. ISBN 9780701180379

Nicholas Stern, *A Blueprint for a Safer Planet: How to manage climate change and create a new era of progress and prosperity*, London, Bodley Head, 2009. ISBN 9781847920379

David Thomas, 'The Mineral Depletion of Foods Available to Us as a Nation (1940–2002) – A Review of the 6th Edition of McCance and Widdowson', *Nutrition and Health*, Vol. 19, 2007, pp.21–55. 0260–1060/07

D'Arcy Thompson, *On Growth and Form*, abridged edition, edited by John Tyler Bonner, Cambridge, Cambridge University Press, 1961. ISBN 0 521 09390 2

J. Scott Turner, *The Extended Organism: the Physiology of Animal-Built Structures*, Cambridge, Massachusetts/London, Harvard University Press, 2000

J. F. V. Vincent, 'Deployable Structures in Nature', listed as a document from the Centre for Biomimetics, The University of Reading, UK, but accessed from University of Bath, Biomimetics and Natural Technologies website. http://www.bath.ac.uk/mech-eng/biomimetics/DeployableStructs.pdf (retrieved 21.01.11)

J. F. V. Vincent, 'Survival of the cheapest', *Materials Today*, December 2002, pp.28–41

J. F. V. Vincent, 'Biomimetics: a review', *Proc. IMechE Part H: J. Proceedings Engineering in Medicine*, 223, 919–39

J. F. V. Vincent and P. Owers, 'Mechanical design of hedgehog spines and porcupine quills', *Journal of Zoology*, 210, pp.55–75

Steven Vogel, *Life in Moving Fluids: The Physical Biology of Flow*, Chichester, West Sussex, Princeton University Press, 1994. ISBN 0-691-02616-5

Steven Vogel, *Cats' Paws and Catapults: Mechanical worlds of Nature and People*, New York, W. W. Norton & Company, 1998. ISBN 0-393-04641-9

Robert Webb, 'Offices that breathe naturally', *New Scientist*, issue 1929, 11 June 1994.

T. H. Wegner and P. E. Jones, 'Advancing cellulose-based nanotechnology', *Cellulose* (2006) 13:115 –18

Edward O. Wilson, *Biophilia*, Cambridge, Massachusetts, Harvard University Press, 1984. ISBN 0-674-07442-4

J. Woodhuysen and J. Kaplinsky, *Energise*, London, Beautiful Books Limited, 2009. ISBN 9781905636273

Broadcasts / videos / talks

Steve Corbett, Green Oak Carpentry, talk delivered at the launch of the 2011 Wood Awards, The Building Centre, London, 24 March 2011

Henk Jonkers, *Material World*, BBC Radio 4, 3.30pm, 2 September 2010; programme about self-repairing concrete

Hans Rosling, 'Hans Rosling on global population growth', TED talk, filmed June 2010, posted July 2010. http://www.ted.com/talks/hans_rosling_on_global_population_growth.html

Paul Stamets, 'Six ways that mushrooms can save the world', TED Talk, filmed March 2008, posted May 2008. http://www.ted.com/talks/paul_stamets_on_6_ways_mushrooms_can_save_the_world.html

Interviews

Patrick Bellew, interview 9 December 2010

David Crooks, interview 3 December 2010

Simon Guest, telephone interview, 8 February 2011

Peter Head and Malcolm Smith, interview 22 December 2010

Neil Thomas, interview 1 February 2010

Tonkin Liu Architects, interview 17 December 2010

Julian Vincent, numerous meetings and telephone conversations

Websites

Competence Centre, Berlin Water Company: http://www.kompetenz-wasser.de/SCST.22.0.html?&L=1&type=title%3Daccelerate

BioPower Systems Pty Ltd: www.biopowersystems.com

Carbon8: http://www.c8s.co.uk/technology.php

Andres Harris, Architect: http://www.andres.harris.cl/?page_id=156

International Energy Agency (key world energy statistics): http://www.iea.org/textbase/nppdf/free/2010/key_stats_2010.pdf

Living Machines (water treatment systems): http://www.livingmachines.com/ (accessed 25.01.11)

SolaRoof (bubble insulated roof technology): http://www.solaroof.org/wiki/SolaRoof/SolaRoofTech (accessed 25.01.11)

Notes

1   The origins of the term are described in some detail by Bernadette Bensaude-Vincent, Hervé Arribart, Yves Bouligand and Clément Sanchez in 'Chemists and the school of nature', *New Journal of Chemistry*, 26, 2002, pp.1–5.

2   Quoted in Hugh Aldersey-Williams, *Zoomorphic: New Animal Architecture*, London, Laurence King, 2003, p.22.

3   Quoted during course at Schumacher College, 'Natural Capitalism', delivered by Janine Benyus and Amory Lovins, 23–26 September 2003. Note that Janine Benyus more recently refers to 'life's genius' rather than 'nature's genius': http://www.biomimicryinstitute.org/about-us/what-is-biomimicry.html (accessed 04.07.11).

4   Edward O. Wilson, *Biophilia*, Harvard University Press, Cambridge, Massachusetts, 1984.

5   Steven Vogel explores this issue at some length in *Cat's Paws and Catapults: Mechanical worlds of Nature and People*, New York, W. W. Norton & Company, 1998, pp.18 and 300.

6   The claims for the distances over which the beetle can detect a forest fire vary wildly, with some sources claiming up to 80 km (David Grimm, 'Beetles may help battle blazes', *Science*, 13 August 2004, Vol. 305, p. 940 – retrieved from www.sciencemag.org on 28.03.11), while others claim 10 km (Kathryn Phillips, 'Beetles "hear" heat through pressure vessels', *Journal of Experimental Biology*, first published online 8 August 2008) and others still refer to distances of 1 km (D. X. Hammer, H. Schmitz, A. Schmitz, Rylander, H. Grady and A. J. Welch, 'Sensitivity threshold and response characteristics of infrared detection in the beetle Melanophila acuminata (Coleoptera: Buprestidae)', *Comparative Biochemistry and Physiology - Part A: Molecular & Integrative Physiology* 128, pp.805-19). I have used the 10 km figure.

7   Vogel, *Cats' Paws, op. cit.* explores this issue at some length in Chapter 12. I have summarised from his excellent description of historical examples.

8   J. F. V. Vincent, and M. J. King, 'The mechanism of drilling by wood wasp ovipositors', *Biomimetics* 3, pp.187–201.

9   J. F. V. Vincent and P. Owers, 'Mechanical design of hedgehog spines and porcupine quills', *Journal of Zoology* 210, 1986. pp.55–75.

10   I am grateful to Adriaan Beukers and Ed van Hinte for allowing me to produce this illustration based on their work in A. Beukers and E. van Hinte, *Lightness: The inevitable renaissance of minimum energy structures*, Rotterdam, 010 Publishers, 1999.

11   'Considerations on the architecture of our time' – Transcript of the British Italian Society Leconfield Lecture by Pier Luigi Nervi.

12   Quoted in obituary in *The Daily Telegraph*, 10 January 1979 – original source not given.

13   Some gridshells have achieved factor-15 savings in resource use. The Weald and Downland Gridshell by Edward Cullinan Architects with Buro Happold and Green Oak Carpentry weighed only 6 tonnes compared to an estimated 100 tonnes for a traditional barn of equivalent size. Source: Steve Corbett, Green Oak Carpentry, Launch of the 2011 Wood Awards, The Building Centre, 24 March 2011.

14   Quoted in Mike Hansell, *Animal Architecture (Oxford Animal Biology Series)*, Oxford, Oxford University Press, 2005, p.145.

15   Andres Harris, Architect: http://www.andres.harris.cl/?page_id=156 (retrieved 13.02.10).

16   See Claus C. Mattheck, *Design in Nature – Learning from trees*, Berlin/Heidelberg/New York, Springer-Verlag, 1998.

17   Vogel, *Cats' Paws, op. cit.*, pp. 431–2.

18   'Buttress' is the normal way people refer to these tree structures, but it is a misnomer because they actually work in tension rather than compression. Just as with a guy rope, shifting the connection point further from the base of the upright gives greater resistance to overturning.

19   Hansell, *Animal Architecture, op. cit.*, p.134.

20   Otto, et al., *Institute for Lightweight Structures volumes IL1 to IL32* (dates from 1971), published by Institut für leichte Flächentragwerke, Universität Stuttgart, School of Architecture and Building Engineering, University of Bath, Universität Essen, Gesamthochschule, Fachbereich Bauwesen.

21   'Anticlastic' is a term that refers to a surface that is curved in opposite ways in two directions like a saddle.

22   Vogel, *Cats' Paws, op. cit.*, p.148.

23   Refer to Julian Vincent's paper 'Deployable Structures in Nature', listed as a document from the Centre for Biomimetics, The University of Reading, but accessed from University of Bath, Biomimetics and Natural Technologies website http://www.bath.ac.uk/mech-eng/biomimetics/DeployableStructs.pdf (retrieved 21.01.11).

24   See Chilton, et al., 'Morphology of Some Three-Dimensional Beam Grillage Structures in Architecture and Nature', *Natürliche Konstruktionen 9, Evolution of Natural Structures*, Third International Symposium of Sonderforschungsbereich 230, Stuttgart, pp.19-24.

25   Mike Hansell, *Built by Animals: The Natural History of Animal Architecture*, Oxford, Oxford University Press, 2007, pp.76–7.

26   Ibid., pp.19–20.

27   Tom Mueller, 'Biomimetics', *National Geographic*, April 2008. http://ngm.nationalgeographic.com/2008/04/biomimetics/tom-mueller-text/1 (accessed 03.04.11)

28   Janine Benyus, *Biomimicry: Innovation Inspired by Nature*, New York, Harper Collins, 1998, p.97.

29 J. F. V. Vincent, 'Biomimetics: a review', *Proc. IMechE Part H: J. Engineering in Medicine*, 223, 919–39.

30 Three European studies show very consistent trends of an approximate 50 per cent decline in sperm counts in European males since 1938. These are summarised, together with other studies, by Shiva Dindyal MBBS (London) BSc. (Hons) Imperial College School of Medicine, 'The sperm count has been decreasing steadily for many years in Western industrialised countries: Is there an endocrine basis for this decrease?' *The Internet Journal of Urology*, Volume 2 Number 1, 2004, http://www.ispub.com/ostia/index.php?xmlFilePath=journals/iju/vol2n1/sperm.xml (retrieved on 24.01.11)

31 Much of this section is based on unpublished work by Graham Dodd of Arup Research and Development.

32 Hansell, *Built*, *op. cit.*, p.75.

33 'Thixotropy' is defined in Chambers dictionary as 'the property of showing a temporary reduction in viscosity when shaken or stirred'. An example can be found by standing at the shoreline of a beach and vibrating your foot in the sand. Seawater flows between the sand particles such that the combination behaves like a liquid and your foot can be easily pushed down into the sand. If you stop vibrating your foot, the sand immediately returns to a solid state.

34 Robert Allen (ed.), *Bulletproof Feathers: How Science Uses Nature's Secrets to Design Cutting-Edge Technology*, Chicago and London, University of Chicago Press, 2010. Refer to chapter by Vincent, p.134.

35 J. E. Gordon, *The New Science of Strong Materials*, London, Penguin Books Ltd, Second Edition, 1976, p.118.

36 Tom Shelley, 'Rapid manufacturing set to go mainstream', *Eureka* magazine, 14 November 2007. http://www.eurekamagazine.co.uk/article/12049/Rapid-manufacturing-set-to-go-mainstream.aspx (accessed 03.04.11).

37 T. H. Wegner and P. E. Jones, 'Advancing cellulose-based nanotechnology', *Cellulose* (2006) 13:115–18.

38 I have only been able to source popular science articles and an abstract submitted by Dosier (G. K. Dosier, 'Biologically Manufactured Building Materials', an abstract submitted for 'Geobiology in Space Exploration' Workshop at Université Cady Ayyad, Ibn Battuta Centre, Morocco on 19 January 2011. http://www.irsps.unich.it/education/geoexp2011/form/abstract1.php?absrd2011+46 (retrieved 02.04.11). Some writers have claimed that the process emits substantial quantities of ammonia as a by-product, which could prove to be problematic.

39 Dr. Carolyn Dry, 'Development of self-repairing concrete', Natural Process Design Inc. website (accessed 24.01.11) http://www.naturalprocessdesign.com/Tech_Concrete.htm.

40 H. Jonkers, 'Bioconcrete', Technical University of Delft website (accessed 24.01.11). http://www.tnw.tudelft.nl/live/pagina.jsp?id=6ce46115-d4b8-4668-a1a4-74c09b6d34ee&lang=en

41 If we attempt to quantify the energy savings achievable, we could compare the embodied energy of, say, aluminium with wood and then assume that rapid manufacturing with cellulose could create structural elements with, as an educated guess, a sixth of the embodied energy of a solid timber section. The diagrams earlier in the chapter explaining shape and hierarchy showed that it is relatively straightforward to reduce the weight of an element to 14 per cent or even 5 per cent of its original mass. We then need to assume a certain amount of energy involved in the RM process itself. A factor-6 saving for RM manufacturing with cellulose relative to solid timber feels relatively conservative. Using embodied-energy figures (from Prof. Geoff Hammond, Craig Jones, Sustainable Energy Research Team, Department of Mechanical Engineering, Bath University, 'Inventory of Carbon and Energy (ICE). Version 1.6a' http://www.bath.ac.uk/mech-eng/sert/embodied/) of 157.1 MJ/kg for aluminium and 9.4 MJ/kg for timber, and the assumed efficiencies achieved through RM, this would suggest an embodied-energy reduction from 157.1 down to 1.57 MJ/kg (a factor-100 increase in resource efficiency).

42 Allen (ed.), *op. cit.*, refer to chapter by Vincent, pp.134–71.

43 The original source for this remark is Justus von Liebig in *Agriculturchemie*. The historical debate about London's sewers is described at some length by Carolyn Steel in *Hungry City*, London, Chatto & Windus, 2008, pp.249–81; and by Herbert Girardet in *Cities, People, Planet: Liveable cities for a sustainable world*, Chichester, West Sussex, John Wiley & Sons, 2004, p.77.

44 Lovins, 'Natural Capitalism' course, *op. cit.* Also in Benyus, *Biomimicry*, *op. cit.*

45 Benyus, 'Natural Capitalism' course, *op. cit.* Also in Benyus, *Biomimicry*, *op. cit.*

46 Benyus, 'Natural Capitalism' course, *op. cit.*

47 There are some limited exceptions to this. Arguably fossil fuels are an example of waste, and it could be seen as ironic that we are currently getting ourselves into difficulties as a direct result of using waste from ancient ecosystems.

48 *Brewing a future* – Zeri Emissions Research Initiative http://www.sdearthtimes.com/et0101/et0101s7.html (retrieved 19.09.10).

49 This work has been pioneered by Prof. Shuting Chang at the Chinese University of Hong Kong. Refer to Gunter Pauli, *The Blue Economy*, Taos, New Mexico, Paradigm Publications, 2010, pp.82–6.

50 Frustratingly, Gunter Pauli does not provide any citations in *The Blue Economy* (*op. cit.*), for the claimed efficiency benefits, so it is difficult to verify the figures.

51 ibid, p.25. The author documents a large number of schemes that have employed these ideas.

52 Steel, *op. cit.* It is difficult to single out particular passages as this is really the essence of the whole book. The concluding chapter on 'Sitopia' provides a useful summary, but the whole book is well worth reading.

53 Desai, Pooran, *One Planet Communities: A real-life guide to sustainable living*, Chichester, West Sussex, John Wiley & Sons Limited, 2010, p.103.

54 'Living machines' is a trademark for a form of biological wastewater treatment initially developed by John Todd and now marketed as a product by Worrell Water Technologies, LC in Charlottesville, Virginia.

55 The technology has been developed by Carbon8, and is undergoing further research and development http://www.c8s.co.uk/technology.php

56 The idea of vertical farms, which has been given extensive coverage in recent years, suffers from exactly these kinds of functional challenges. Agriculture is almost totally dependent on light, and to substitute natural light with artificial light is both a financial and a practical challenge. George Monbiot has commented on the financial realities: http://www.monbiot.com/archives/2010/08/16/towering-lunacy/. The schemes designed by Dickson Despommier show vertical farms supplied with energy from photovoltaic panels, and if one assumed the most efficient PV cells commercially available (about 15 per cent) and factored in the energy losses from the most efficient LED lights then the required area of PV would be roughly ten times the cultivated area of the vertical farm. Consequently, urban farming is only likely to work using natural light, which means either horizontally or using terraces orientated towards the south.

57 Michael Pollan, The Omnivore's Dilemma, London, Bloomsbury Publishing PLC, 2006, pp.67–8.

58 Pauli, op. cit., p.xxxi.

59 Detroit provides a good example of what can happen when a whole city is dependent on one industry. The collapse of car manufacturing has left much of the city as a wasteland.

60 'Peak oil' was a term coined by geologist M. King Hubbert, who studied the productivity of oil wells over time. He found that all followed a bell-curve distribution and that the peak of production was the point at which the economics changed significantly, because from then on there would be steadily decreasing supply coupled with increasing amounts of energy required to extract the oil. Extending the theory to global oil reserves suggested dire economic circumstances once the global peak is reached. Perhaps the most significant thing about peak-oil theory is that it showed persuasively that the point at which the resource peaks is more significant than the point at which it becomes exhausted.

61 The team's analysis extended to far more than water (they analysed the characteristics of the biome in terms of water collection, filtration and storage, solar gain and reflectance, carbon sequestration, evapo-transpiration, nutrient cycling, biodiversity, soil building and temperature amongst many other biological processes) and they applied biomimicry to every aspect of the design process. I have focused on the water story because it is a particularly good example of how to transform a problem of overabundance into an ingenious solution.

62 David Thomas, 'The Mineral Depletion of Foods Available to Us as a Nation (1940–2002) – A Review of the 6th Edition of McCance and Widdowson', Nutrition and Health, Vol. 19, 2007, pp.21–55. 0260–1060/07. http://www.mineralresourcesint.co.uk/pdf/Mineral_Depletion_of_Foods_1940_2002.pdf

63 These already exist and have been implemented on certain pioneering schemes by the Berlin Water Company's Competence Centre http://www.kompetenz-wasser.de/SCST.22.0.html?&L=1&type=title%3Daccelerate

64 Refer to the Living Machines website 'history' page for more information and other pages for further technical detail. http://www.livingmachines.com/about/history/

65 Steven Vogel, Life in Moving Fluids: The Physical Biology of Flow, Chichester, West Sussex, Princeton University Press, 1994, pp.317–21.

66 Jung Yeop Lee and Æ Sang Joon Lee, 'Murray's law and the bifurcation angle in the arterial micro-circulation system and their application to the design of microfluidics', Microfluidics and Nanofluidics, Vol. 8, Number 1, 2010, pp.85–95.

67 Thermophiles live at temperatures above 100 ºC in submarine volcanic vents.

68 Hansell, Animal Architecture, op. cit., p.4.

69 When I say 'loosely', I do not mean this in a highly critical way – only to explain why I have not gone into more detail to explain the source of inspiration and how the function is delivered in nature.

70 A well-known and oft-quoted example of this is the space pen that NASA spent millions of dollars developing. The end result was unwieldy, containing an ink pump to make up for the absence of gravity, and unreliable. The Russians, by contrast, just took a pencil.

71 This was primarily the work of Julian Vincent and his colleagues, Drs Olga and Nikolay Bogatyrev, at the University of Bath. It is not possible to give a full explanation of TRIZ or BioTRIZ in the limited space available in this book, so those intrigued by these powerful methodologies can read more in the chapters written by Julian Vincent in Allen (ed.), op. cit.

72 Robert Webb, 'Offices that breathe naturally', New Scientist, issue 1929, 11 Juen 1994 and J. P. E. C. Darlington, 'The structure of mature mounds of the termite Macrotermes michaelseni in Kenya', Insect Science and its Applications, 6, 1986, pp.149–56.

73 In this vein, anyone interested in making a termite-inspired building would be well advised to read J. Scott Turner and Rupert C. Soar, 'Beyond biomimicry: What termites can tell us about realizing the living building', First International Conference on Industrialized, Intelligent Construction (I3CON), Loughborough University, 14–16 May 2008, and any more recent papers they may have published.

74 ibid.

75 David J. C. MacKay, Sustainable Energy – without the hot air, Cambridge, UIT Cambridge Ltd, 2008.

76 There are a very limited number of exceptions to this, such as thermophiles that have evolved to live in deep-sea volcanic vents.

77 The earth continuously receives about 174,000 Terawatts (TW) of energy from the sun, of which 30 per cent is reflected back into space, 19 per cent is absorbed by clouds and 89,000 TW reaches the surface. Our average annual energy consumption between 2008 and 2010 was very close to 15 TW. The earth therefore receives 11,600 times as much energy as we use, and, at the surface, we receive 5,933 times as much as we consume. Sources: IEA Key World Energy Statistics 2010, http://www.iea.org/textbase/nppdf/free/2010/key_stats_2010.pdf; Wikipedia, http://en.wikipedia.org/wiki/World_energy_consumption#cite_note-EIA-0

78 MacKay, *op. cit.*

79 One of the most thorough and impartial assessments of energy options is MacKay, *op. cit.*

80 Derek Abbott, 'Keeping the Energy Debate Clean: How Do We Supply the World's Energy Needs?' Proceedings of the IEEE, Vol. 98, No. 1, January 2010, pp.42–66.

81 Hermann Scheer, *The Solar Economy: Renewable Energy for a Sustainable Global Future*, London, Earthscan, 2002.

82 Strictly speaking, geothermal energy is not renewable but the size of the resource compared to the most optimistic rate at which we could extract the energy would still result in the source lasting for hundreds of millions of years.

83 Anon (no author credit), 'Whales and dolphins influence new wind turbine design', *Science Daily*®, 8 July 2008. http://www.sciencedaily.com/releases/2008/07/080707222315.htm

84 Vogel, *Cats' Paws, op. cit.*, pp.96–100.

85 If the blades deflected along their length, then clearly they would need to be on the downwind side of the mast in order to avoid fouling.

86 Anon (no author credit), 'Offshore Wind Power and Wave Energy Devices Create Artificial Reefs' *Science Daily*®, 19 January 2010.

87 Source: http://www.worldometers.info/cars/

88 Source: http://en.wikipedia.org/wiki/shipbuilding

89 Some readers might legitimately question the economic viability of creating the solar economy. The economic situation is complicated by a number of factors. We will need to spend large sums anyway on upgrading our creaking grids and power stations. Appropriate investment in research and development, coupled with economies from scaling up manufacturing and deployment of renewable technologies, would radically reduce costs. We also need to consider which costs are externalised from conventional sources of energy (the damage cost of carbon emissions and the cost of oil-related military operations, to name just two) and what benefits are generally overlooked in renewable-energy technologies. A full economic assessment would need to take account of all these issues. The obstacles to creating the solar economy are mainly political, and initiatives like the Mediterranean Solar Plan are the first signs of what will hopefully gather great momentum.

90 This anecdote was relayed to me by Professor Patrick Hodgkinson, and between his retelling and mine it may be that some inaccuracies have crept in.

91 I have paraphrased the description that Herbert Girardet gives in *Cities, People, Planet, op. cit.*, pp.45–6.

92 See A. E. Seago, P.,Brady, J-P. Vigneron and T. D. Schultz, 'Gold bugs and beyond: a review of iridescence and structural colour mechanisms in beetles (Coleoptera)', *Journal of the Royal Society Interface*, 6, 2009, S165–S184, doi:10.1098/rsif.2008.0354.focus. Published online 28 October 2008.

93 Benyus, *Biomimicry, op. cit.*, pp.253–4.

94 Within the limitations of this book it is not possible to do justice to the depth of thought and design input that the Arup team invested in Dong Tan and Wanzhuang, so I would encourage those readers that want to find out more to read Peter Head, 'The Brunel Lecture 2008: Entering the Ecological Age' http://www.arup.com/_assets/_download/72B9BD7D-19BB-316E-40000ADE36037C13.pdf and Benyus, *Biomimicry, op. cit.*, Chapter 7.

95 Ecological footprinting was developed by Mathis Wackernagel – see intro of Head, *op. cit.*

96 ibid., p.61.

97 Girardet, *op. cit.*, p.11.

98 Head, *op. cit.*, p.18.

99 Ray Anderson, *Confessions of a radical industrialist*, London, Random House Business Books, 2009, p.9.

100 *Interface Sustainability Report*, 1997.

101 P. Hawken, A. Lovins and L. H. Lovins, *Natural Capitalism*, New York, Back Bay Books/Little, Brown and Company, 1999, p.133.

102 Anderson, *op. cit.*, p.4.

103 Hawken, Lovins and Lovins made this observation in Hawken, et al., *op. cit.*, p.170.

104 Julian Vincent makes an observation similar to this in 'Survival of the cheapest', *Materials Today*, December 2002, pp.28–9.

105 Hans Rosling, 'Hans Rosling on global population growth', TED talk, filmed June 2010, posted July 2010. http://www.ted.com/talks/hans_rosling_on_global_population_growth.html.

106 Donella Meadows, 'Leverage Points: Places to intervene in a system', Hartland, Vermont, The Sustainability Institute, 1999. Available online at http://www.sustainer.org/pubs/Leverage_Points.pdf

Index

Image credits

Atelier Ten, 90, 98
Iwan Baan, 22
Bill Bachman, 95
Marks Barfield, 28
BioPower Systems Pty Ltd., 104
Toby Burgess, 69
Culmann and J. Wolff, 14
Cynoclub, 54
Daimler AG, 7–8, 31–32
Vicente del Amo, 5
Martin Dohrn, 55
Georgette Douwma, 105
Exploration, 11, 23, 57–58, 63, 91, 94
Exploration Architecture Limited, 38, 72
Eye of Science, cover, 9, 21, 117
Fotolia, 101
FLC/ADAGP and DACS, 4
Vaughan Fleming, 99
Fstockfoto, 59
Future Systems, 33
Gottlieb Paludan Architects, 106
Kari Greer, 116
Grimshaw, 24–25b, 37, 74, 82
Steve Gschmeissner, 1, 88
S.D. Guest and S. Pellegrino, 44
Gert Jan Hageman, 75
Andreas Harris, 27
Henschel and Jocqué, 35
Ken M. Highfill, 60
Hoberman Associates, 46–48
The HOK Planning Group, 83
George Holton, 110
Institut für Leichtbau Entwerfen und Konstruieren ILEK, 26
Interface, 114–115
Kevin Jarratt, 13
Judit Kimpian, 39–40
Aron Kohr, 78
Dennis Kunkel Microscopy, Inc., 53
Magnus Larsson, 65
Maceo, 12
Claus Matheck, 30
NASA, 100, 107
Susumu Nishinaga, 62, 85
Duncan Noakes, 93
Claude Nuridsany & Marie Perennou, 45
Yoshiharu Matsumura, 17
Matthew Oldfield Photography, 70
Rubik Oleg, 6
Yaniv Peer & Filippo Privitali, 76
Sergio Poretti, 20

Power and Syred, 87
O. Prochnow, 16
Bogo Rasch, 49
Dr Morley Read, 34
Steffen Reichert and Prof. Achim Menges, 66–67
Reid & Peck, 51
RIBA Library Photographs Collection, 3, 36
Professor A. Robinson, 15
Paolo Rosselli, 29
Paula J. Rudall, 61
The Sahara Forest Project Foundation, 108
Seawater Greenhouse Ltd., 80–81
Sebtoja, 50
Scott Sinklier, 77
Tanja Soeter, 64
Steve Speller, 41–43
Joanne Stemberger, 86
Ezra Stoller, 2
Barbara Strnadova, 109
Joseph Subirana, 103
Jerry Tate Architects, 92
Barney Taxel, 84
Kenneth H. Thomas, 56
Tonkin Liu Architects, 18–19, 112–113
Travel The Unknown, 68
Masa Ushioda, 102
Nick Veasey, 10
Vyonyx, 111
Danny Wicke, 73
Wilkinson Eyre Architects, 97
Uwe Wittbrock, 71
Woodland Burial Parks, 52
Alejandro Zaera-Polo and Farshid Moussavi, 89
Solvin Zankl, 79

Note

The author and publisher have made every effort to contact copyright holders and will be happy to correct, in subsequent editions, any errors or omissions that are brought to their attention.